Book 1

The relief teacher toolkit

Cross-curricular activities

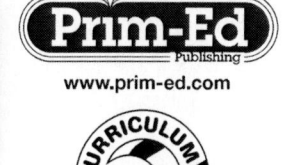

Prim-Ed Publishing
www.prim-ed.com

CURRICULUM LINKED

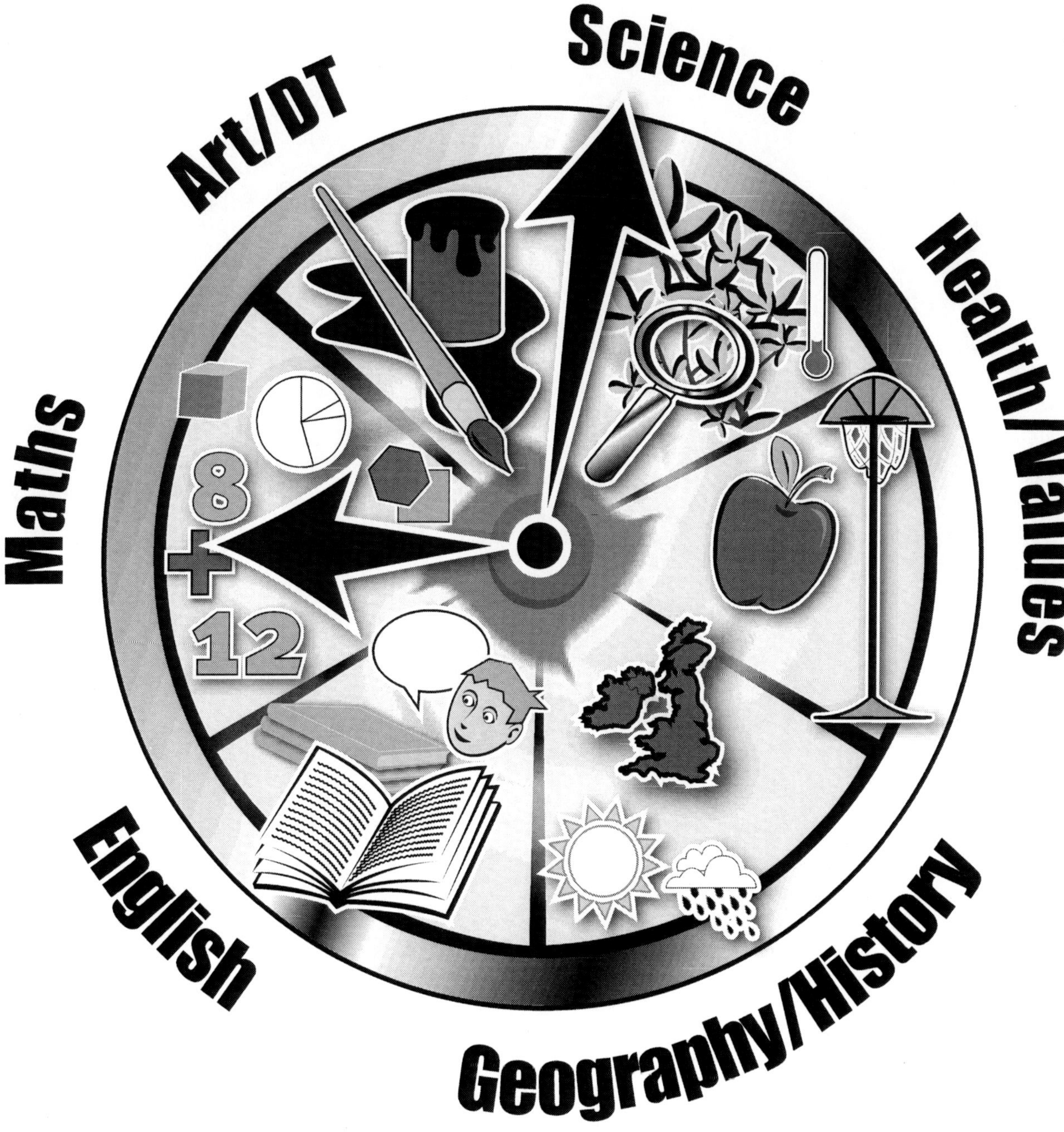
Science
Health/Values
Geography/History
English
Maths
Art/DT
8
+
12

by Kevin Rigg

0756C

THE RELIEF TEACHER TOOLKIT *(Book 1)*

Published by Prim-Ed Publishing 2007
Copyright© Kevin Rigg 2005
ISBN 978 1 84654 077 6
PR–0756

Additional titles available in this series:
THE RELIEF TEACHER TOOLKIT *(Book 2)*
THE RELIEF TEACHER TOOLKIT *(Book 3)*
THE RELIEF TEACHER TOOLKIT *(Book 4)*

Internet websites
In some cases, websites or specific URLs may be recommended. While these are checked and rechecked at the time of publication, the publisher has no control over any subsequent changes which may be made to webpages. It is *strongly* recommended that the class teacher checks *all* URLs before allowing pupils to access them.

View all pages online

Website: www.prim-ed.com

Email: sales@prim-ed.com

Foreword

The relief teacher toolkit is a series of four books which provide convenient resources to assist relief teachers with classroom planning and organisation on a long-term basis. The photocopiable worksheets cover the learning areas of English, mathematics, science, health/values, geography/history and art/DT. The series is also a valuable resource for the classroom teacher, as the worksheets may be used to introduce, consolidate or assess topics being taught.

Additional titles available in this series:

The relief teacher toolkit (Book 2)
The relief teacher toolkit (Book 3)
The relief teacher toolkit (Book 4)

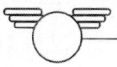

Contents

Teachers notes...iv – vii
Record of worksheet use...............................viii – ix
Blank class record sheet x
Relief teacher survival kit xi

English

Reading/Spelling

1. Animal stories 2–3
2. Make a word 4–5
3. Single sounds read and draw 6–7
4. Ordering 8–9
5. Read and do 10–11
6. Sounds – 1 12–13
7. Sounds – 2 14–15
8. Single sounds – 't' 16–17

Writing

9. My cat 18–19
10. My trip 20–21
11. My news 22–23
12. Recount 24–25

Handwriting

13. Nursery rhyme writing 26–27
14. Drawing nursery rhymes 28–29

Mathematics

Number

15. Numbers 30–31
16. How many? 32–33
17. This old man 34–35

Measurement

18. It's time! 36–37

Shape/Data

19. Circles, squares and triangles 38–39

Science

20. Animal match 40–41
21. Young and adult 42–43
22. The five senses 44–45

Health

23. About your teeth 46–47

Geography/History

24. Wintertime 48–49
25. Summertime 50–51
26. Then and now 52–53
27. A classroom 54–55

Design and technology

28. Build a pumpkin house 56–57
29. Design a building 58–59

Art

30. Wax resist butterflies 60–61
31. Shape collage 62–63

Theme – myself

32. Directed writing – My home/My toys 64–65
33. Body numbers 66–67
34. All about me 68–69
35. My body 70–71
36. Things I like 72–73

Teacher information

The worksheets can all be used as single lessons if time is limited or they may be extended by including some additional activities to expand the topic into other curriculum areas. In some cases, it is possible to develop an entire day's work around one lesson sheet.

The theme pack at the end of each book is an ideal springboard for a long-term relief project, yet each worksheet within the theme pack can stand alone as an individual lesson. The 'Myself' theme pack in this book covers the learning areas of English, mathematics, science, health and values.

The lessons have been specifically designed for the targeted age range. Worksheets from the same section of another book in the series may be more appropriate for any pupil who is working at a different level from the rest of the class. In many cases, the worksheets are differentiated by outcome rather than task and so are appropriate for more than one level of ability.

A number of different teaching methods are included throughout the series to assist in the development of a range of skills across all learning areas.

Each lesson has detailed teachers notes which include:
- *learning area covered*
- *objective(s), summarising what the pupils may achieve*
- *a list of resources required, beyond those normally available in the classroom*
- *specific websites relevant to the activity, where appropriate*
- *a detailed lesson plan, including ideas for classroom organisation*
- *additional activities which extend the theme and expand it into other curriculum areas, including ideas for display*
- *answers, where necessary*
- *curriculum links covered by the activity.*

A printed record sheet is provided for the teacher to keep account of which lessons have been completed with specific classes. A blank copy of the sheet is also included for the teacher to keep his/her own records.

If the worksheets are used for assessment purposes, the lesson plan and organisation provided on the teachers page may not be appropriate and an alternative strategy may need to be employed.

It is assumed that normal classroom stationery and basic art and craft resources are readily available; for example, pencils, scissors and glue.

Some lessons require the pupils to access information and resources from home. Such cases should be communicated to the pupils prior to the day of the lesson.

When possible, audio and video recordings could be made and photographs taken, to increase pupil motivation and encourage them to perform at their best level. These may be used as evidence of work, and as resources to be used at other times. The photographs may be used to enhance displays of work.

It is recommended that relief teachers keep a selection of samples of work from this book as a record of their relief teaching experience.

Display/Presentation ideas

Teachers completing a short term of relief teaching may not find it necessary to display worksheets from these books. However, teachers completing long-term relief, or classroom teachers, may find some of these display/presentation ideas useful:

- *Staple worksheets back to back and hang over string/wire suspended across the room.*
- *Select the most appropriate worksheets to display around a shape, poster, rhyme or picture relating to the worksheets.*
- *Combine all the worksheets to form a book with a cover for the class library.*
- *Display worksheets with artworks by selected pupils.*
- *Fix worksheets to an appropriate frieze painted by the pupils.*
- *Pupils decorate the border of the worksheet with relevant shapes or pictures.*
- *Pupils create an artwork or shape relevant to the worksheet and attach their worksheet to it. The artwork/shape should be larger than the worksheet (A3 size); for example, when pupils are completing the worksheet about 'ee', they may draw or make and cut out a 'tree' or 'bee' shape for their worksheet.*

The relief teacher toolkit
Prim-Ed Publishing   www.prim-ed.com

Teacher pages

A teacher page accompanies each pupil worksheet. It provides the following information:

The symbol at the top indicates the learning area.

The title indicates the activity being covered.

The objective(s) summarise what the pupils may achieve on completion of the task.

Specific websites have been included where appropriate. Pupils may also use a search engine to find information from the Internet on a particular topic.

The resources list those requirements for the task which might not normally be readily available in the classroom. Teachers may select those which are appropriate or easy to obtain.

These may include items and information which pupils bring from home, library resources on a particular topic, magazines for cutting out pictures, literature relevant to the activity, prepared work and resources to demonstrate what is required from pupils or to help with class discussion. Any prepared work and resources may be kept and used for future lessons.

The additional activities provide suggestions for extending the activity and expanding it into other curriculum areas.

These activities include suggestions for display, ideas for research and projects, designing and playing games, dramatising roles, conducting surveys and presenting results graphically.

The lesson plan and organisation provides a detailed structure for the lesson and ideas for classroom organisation.

Most lessons begin with a discussion to determine how much the pupils already know about the subject. Some resources may be used at this stage to enhance discussion.

Reading through the worksheet with the pupils ensures they understand what is required of them. Allowing pupils to work in small groups to discuss their work and, where necessary, to prepare and edit drafts, gives them the opportunity to learn from one another.

The answers are provided as necessary. In many cases, it is expected that the pupils' work will be teacher checked.

The curriculum links covered by each activity are provided for each country.

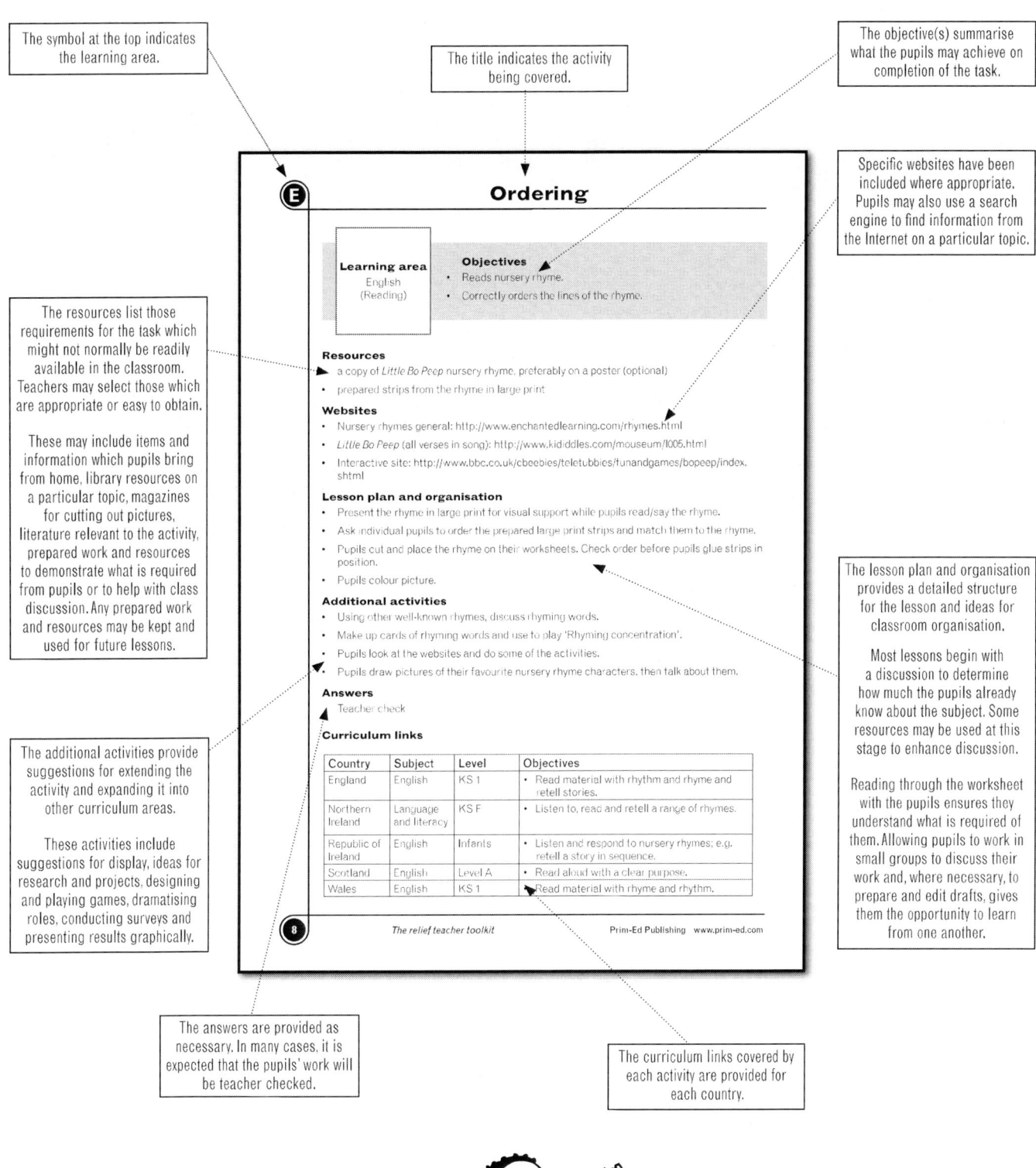

Ordering

Learning area
English
(Reading)

Objectives
• Reads nursery rhyme.
• Correctly orders the lines of the rhyme.

Resources
• a copy of *Little Bo Peep* nursery rhyme, preferably on a poster (optional)
• prepared strips from the rhyme in large print

Websites
• Nursery rhymes general: http://www.enchantedlearning.com/rhymes.html
• *Little Bo Peep* (all verses in song): http://www.kididdles.com/mouseum/l005.html
• Interactive site: http://www.bbc.co.uk/cbeebies/teletubbies/funandgames/bopeep/index.shtml

Lesson plan and organisation
• Present the rhyme in large print for visual support while pupils read/say the rhyme.
• Ask individual pupils to order the prepared large print strips and match them to the rhyme.
• Pupils cut and place the rhyme on their worksheets. Check order before pupils glue strips in position.
• Pupils colour picture.

Additional activities
• Using other well-known rhymes, discuss rhyming words.
• Make up cards of rhyming words and use to play 'Rhyming concentration'.
• Pupils look at the websites and do some of the activities.
• Pupils draw pictures of their favourite nursery rhyme characters, then talk about them.

Answers
Teacher check

Curriculum links

Country	Subject	Level	Objectives
England	English	KS 1	• Read material with rhythm and rhyme and retell stories.
Northern Ireland	Language and literacy	KS F	• Listen to, read and retell a range of rhymes.
Republic of Ireland	English	Infants	• Listen and respond to nursery rhymes; e.g. retell a story in sequence.
Scotland	English	Level A	• Read aloud with a clear purpose.
Wales	English	KS 1	• Read material with rhyme and rhythm.

8   *The relief teacher toolkit*   Prim-Ed Publishing   www.prim-ed.com

Pupil worksheets

The pupil worksheets provide a range of activities to assist in the development of skills across all learning areas of the curriculum.

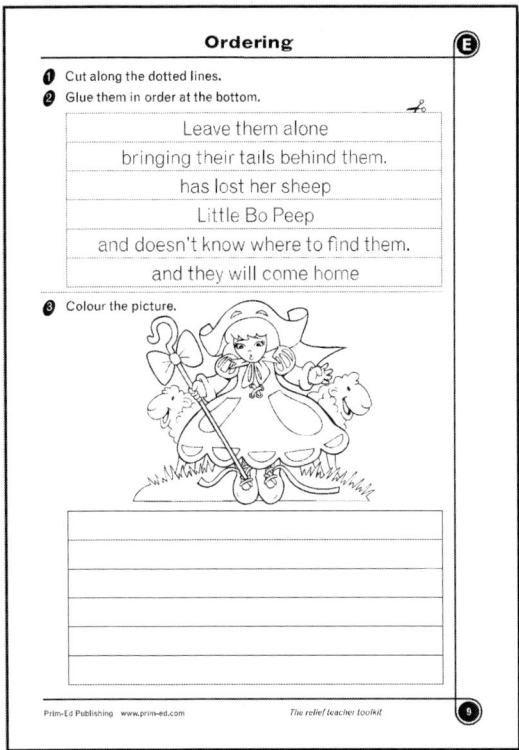

English
Ordering (page 9)
Pupils cut out individual lines of a well-known rhyme which has been jumbled up. They place the lines in the correct order and glue them in place.

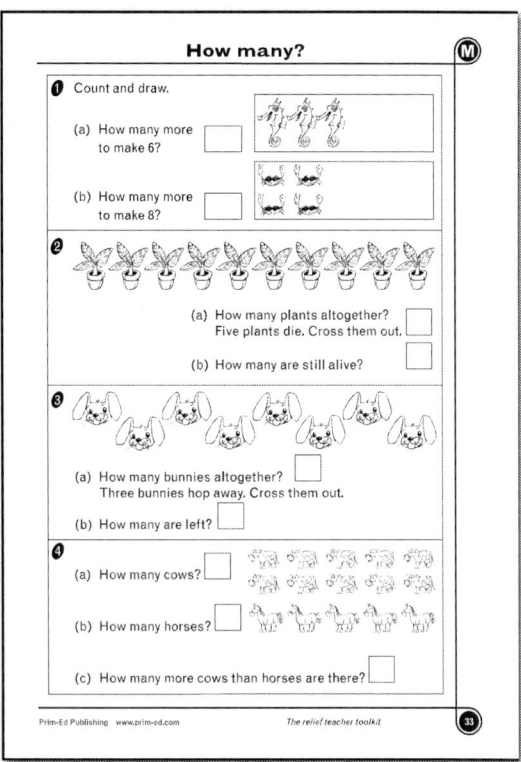

Mathematics
How many? (page 33)
Counting objects to answer addition and subtraction problems.

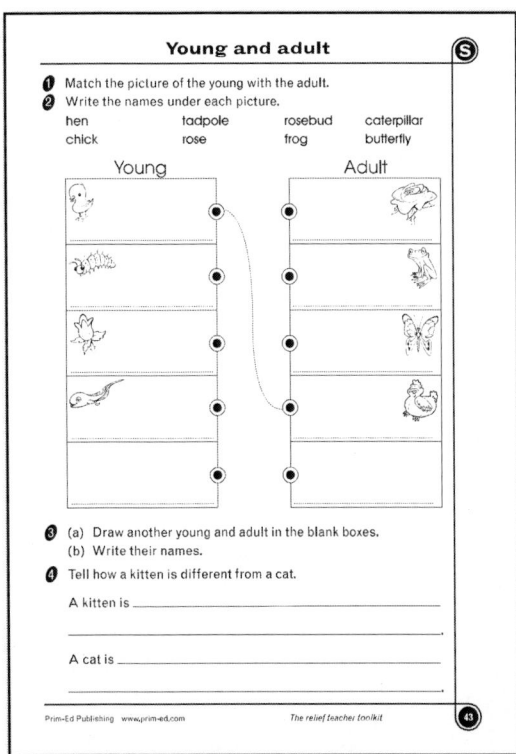

Science
Young and adult (page 43)
Pupils demonstrate their awareness of living things and recognise the changes that occur from young to adult.

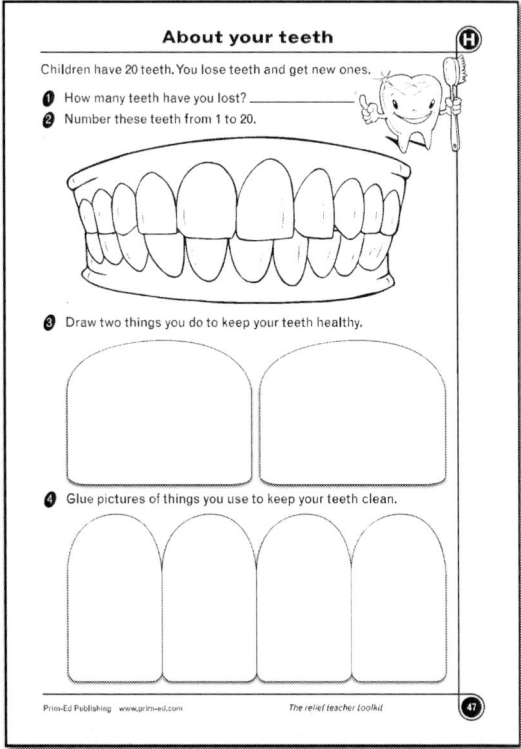

Health
About your teeth (page 47)
Pupils appreciate the need for oral hygiene and recognise ways to keep their teeth clean and healthy.

Pupil worksheets

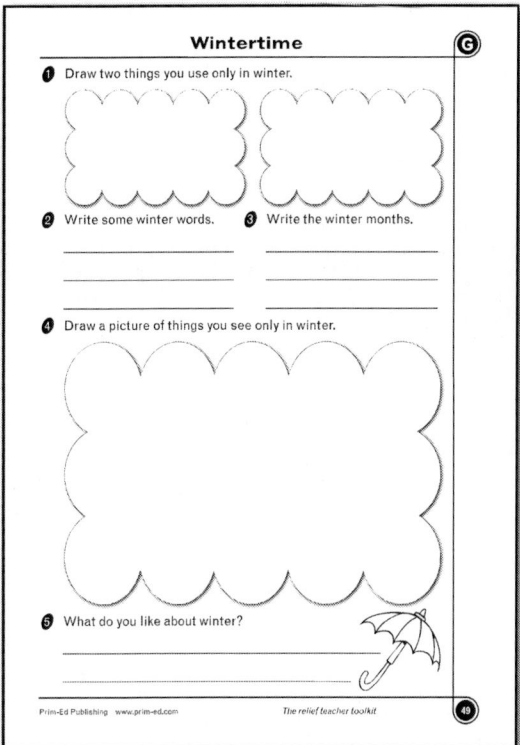

Geography
Wintertime (page 49)
Pupils demonstrate their awareness of the natural changes that occur with the seasons and how these affect their life.

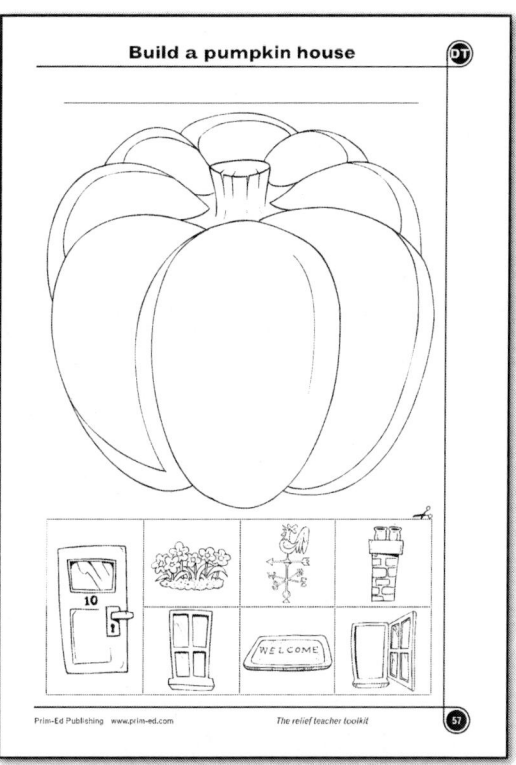

Design and technology
Build a pumpkin house (page 57)
Pupils design a 'pumpkin house', choosing where to place features such as doors and windows.

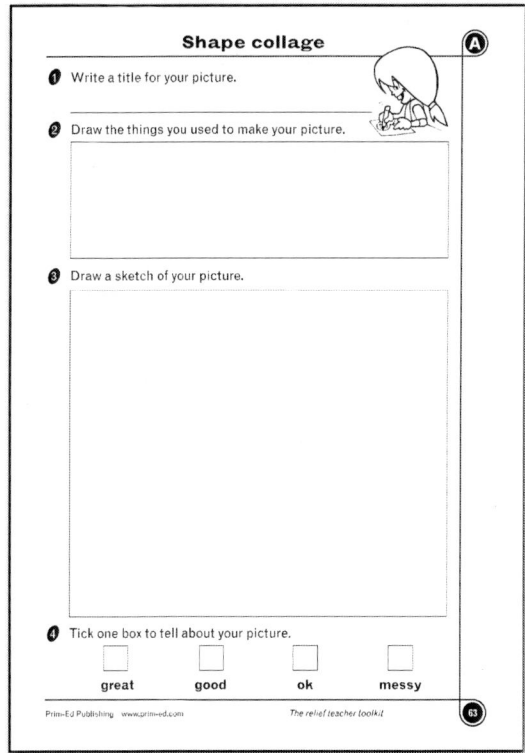

Art
Shape collage (page 63)
Pupils make a collage using 2-D shapes of different sizes. They evaluate their own work.

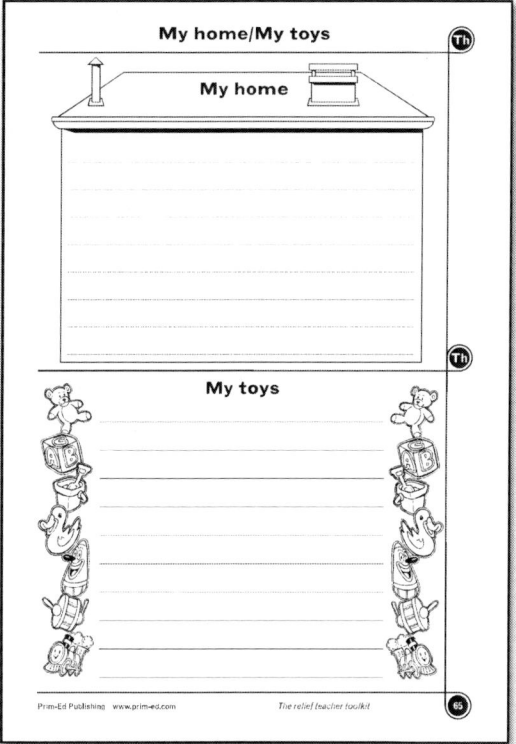

The theme pack 'Myself'
My home/My toys (page 65)
Pupils record what makes their house a home—who lives with them and the activities they share. They also describe their favourite toys, explaining why they are special.

Class record sheet

Teacher's name: _____

	Title of lesson	School:				School:			
		Class:	Class:	Class:	Class:	Class:	Class:	Class:	Class:
1.	Animal stories								
2.	Make a word								
3.	Single sounds read and draw								
4.	Ordering								
5.	Read and do								
6.	Sounds (1)								
7.	Sounds (2)								
8.	Single sounds – 't'								
9.	My cat								
10.	My trip								
11.	My news								
12.	Recount								
13.	Nursery rhyme writing								
14.	Drawing nursery rhymes								
15.	Numbers								
16.	How many?								
17.	This old man								
18.	It's time!								

The relief teacher toolkit

Prim-Ed Publishing   www.prim-ed.com

Class record sheet

School: _____ Teacher's name: _____

Title of lesson		Class:	Class:	Class:	Class:	Class:	Class:	Class:	Class:
19.	Circles, squares and triangles								
20.	Animal match								
21.	Young and adult								
22.	The five senses								
23.	About your teeth								
24.	Wintertime								
25.	Summertime								
26.	Then and now								
27.	A classroom								
28.	Build a pumpkin house								
29.	Design a building								
30.	Wax resist butterflies								
31.	Shape collage								
32.	Directed writing								
33.	Body numbers								
34.	All about me								
35.	My body								
36.	Things I like								

Class record sheet

Teacher's name: _____

Title of lesson	School:							School:							
	Class:	Class:	Class:	Class:	Class:			Class:	Class:	Class:	Class:	Class:			

The relief teacher toolkit

Prim-Ed Publishing   www.prim-ed.com

Relief teacher survival kit

Every relief teacher should have a supply of resources packed and ready to go. These should include:

Resource	Tick box
Rewards such as stickers, coloured dots, stamps etc.	
Stories appropriate to each year level; for example, Roald Dahl's 'Revolting rhymes'	
A collection of **poems**, **singing games** and **songs** for lesson breaks, attention-gaining and settling purposes	
Story tapes/CDs may also be useful for settling pupils, to reward pupils for good behaviour (who may serve as page-turners) or to allow the teacher to rest his/her voice or to observe the pupils	
Pens and pencils for marking work	
A collection of 'busy-work' sheets, such as word searches, crosswords or intricate shape pattern sheets to colour for early finishers	
A name badge	
A whistle for duty and/or PE .	
A labelled mug for tea or coffee	
Some games to teach the pupils, such as 'Hangman'	
A collection of 30 or more interesting pictures to use as motivation for story writing	

Relief teachers should keep resources relevant to specific worksheets in a folder or plastic sleeve to enable them to find them easily.

The relief teacher toolkit

Animal stories

Learning area
English (Reading)

Objectives
- Recognises words relating to animals.
- Describes different animals.
- Categorises animals using different criteria.

Resources
- pictures of various dogs, cats, birds and fish
- range of reference material and literature about animals

Lesson plan and organisation
- Look at the pictures and reference books on the animals, discussing their physical appearances and characteristics.
- Around a picture of each animal, write vocabulary relating to it; e.g. how it moves, sounds, behaves. Pupils move like various animals as indicated.
- Compare animals with one another, categorising them in different ways, examining similarities and differences.
- Pupils complete worksheets.

Additional activities
- Pupils orally present their own *Who am I?* riddles to the class. Pupils illustrate answers.
- Pupils dramatise animal actions.
- List animal action words as suggested by the pupils.

Answers
1. (a) bark (b) swim (c) fly (d) purr
2. (a) bird (b) fish

Curriculum links

Country	Subject	Level	Objectives
England	English	KS 1	• Develop contextual understanding and focus on meaning derived from text.
Northern Ireland	Language and literacy	KS F	• Use text to make predictions.
Republic of Ireland	English	Infants	• Encounter early reading.
Scotland	English	Level A	• Read simple information.
Wales	English	KS 1	• Develop contextual understanding and focus on meaning derived from text.

The relief teacher toolkit   Prim-Ed Publishing   www.prim-ed.com

Animal stories

1 Write the best word for each sentence.

purr   bark   fly   swim

(a) A dog can _____ .

(b) A fish can _____ .

(c) A bird can _____ .

(d) A cat can _____ .

2 Who am I? Draw the animal.

(a) I can fly.

I have wings.

I lay eggs.

I am a _____ .

(b) I live in water.

I can swim.

I have fins.

I am a _____ .

Make a word

Learning area	Objectives
English (Reading and spelling)	• Understands that 'ea' and 'ee' make the same sound. • Learns which words require 'ee' and 'ea'. • Knows that words are incorrectly spelt if the wrong letters are chosen.

Resources

• prepared demonstration cards with the 'ea' and 'ee' sound

Lesson plan and organisation

• This lesson may be taken over two sessions by cutting the worksheet into two.

• Pupils should be familiar with the sounds 'ea' and 'ee' and have prior knowledge of all words to be made. These should be written on the board.

• Practise the sounds with these and other words before pupils attempt the worksheet.

Additional activities

• In groups, pupils find and illustrate other words with 'ea' and 'ee' sounds.

• Pupils make little booklets of words for each sound.

Answers

1. (a) leaf (b) read (c) meat (d) sea

2. (a) tree (b) green (c) feet (d) bee

Curriculum links

Country	Subject	Level	Objectives
England	English	KS 1	• Use simple spelling patterns.
Northern Ireland	Language and literacy	KS F	• Use knowledge of sound-symbol relationships.
Republic of Ireland	English	Infants	• Begin to develop conventional spelling.
Scotland	English	Level A	• Look at patterns within words.
Wales	English	KS 1	• Use simple spelling patterns.

Make a word

1 Cut out each sound and glue it in the space to make a word. Write the word and draw a picture in the box.

2 Cut out each sound and glue it in the space to make a word. Write the word and draw a picture in the box.

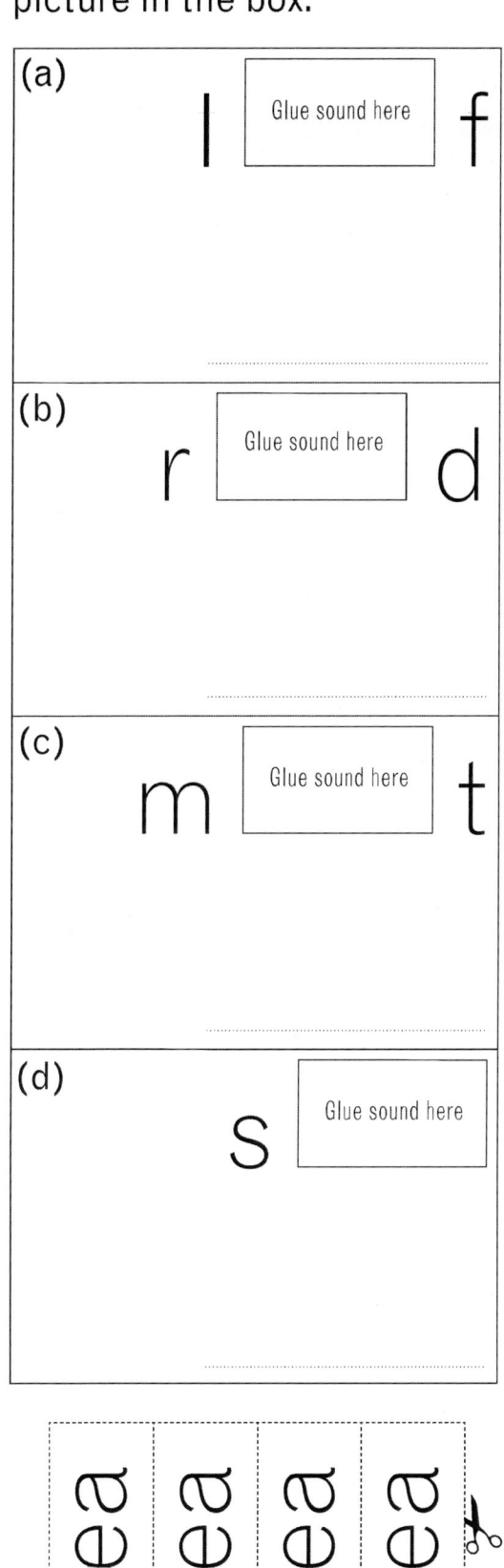

Single sounds read and draw

Learning area
English (Reading and spelling)

Objectives

*   Knows letter sounds.

*   Demonstrates understanding of text.

Resources

*   objects for demonstration

Lesson plan and organisation

*   Write letters and unfinished words on the board.

*   Show objects and say the words. Repeat the words, emphasising final sound. Pupils say which letter is required for each word.

*   Pupils read phrases in Question 2 orally. Choose pupils to use objects to demonstrate the phrases.

*   Pupils complete worksheet.

Additional activities

*   Present more objects with the 'a' and 'i' sounds and ask pupils to say and write the final sounds.

*   Pupils use objects to make up, say, write and illustrate their own phrases.

Answers

1. (a) tap, bat, man, bag (b) bib, zip, pig, lid

2. Teacher check

Curriculum links

Country	Subject	Level	Objectives
England	English	KS 1	• Read familiar words and recognise words with common spelling patterns.
Northern Ireland	Language and literacy	KS F	• Explore features of written language and use reading cues.
Republic of Ireland	English	Infants	• Build up a sight vocabulary and isolate beginning and final sounds in words.
Scotland	English	Level A	• Develop interest in how words sound and patterns within them.
Wales	English	KS 1	• Develop phonic knowledge, focusing on print symbols and sound patterns.

Single sounds read and draw

1 Finish the words:

(a) Use g, p, t, n   (b) Use p, g, b, d

ta _____   bi _____

ba _____   zi _____

ma _____   pi _____

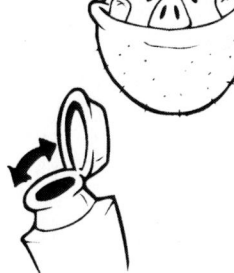

ba _____   li _____

2 Read and draw.

(a)	(b)
a cat on a bat	a bag on a mat
(c)	(d)
a lid on a tin	a bib on a pig

E

| Learning area |
| English (Reading) |

Objectives
- Reads nursery rhyme.
- Correctly orders the lines of the rhyme.

Resources
- a copy of *Little Bo Peep* nursery rhyme, preferably on a poster (optional)
- prepared strips from the rhyme in large print

Websites
- Nursery rhymes general: http://www.enchantedlearning.com/rhymes.html
- *Little Bo Peep* (all verses in song): http://www.kididdles.com/mouseum/l005.html
- Interactive site: http://www.bbc.co.uk/cbeebies/teletubbies/funandgames/bopeep/index.shtml

Lesson plan and organisation
- Present the rhyme in large print for visual support while pupils read/say the rhyme.
- Ask individual pupils to order the prepared large print strips and match them to the rhyme.
- Pupils cut and place the rhyme on their worksheets. Check order before pupils glue strips in position.
- Pupils colour picture.

Additional activities
- Using other well-known rhymes, discuss rhyming words.
- Make up cards of rhyming words and use to play 'Rhyming concentration'.
- Pupils look at the websites and do some of the activities.
- Pupils draw pictures of their favourite nursery rhyme characters, then talk about them.

Answers
Teacher check

Curriculum links

Country	Subject	Level	Objectives
England	English	KS 1	• Read material with rhythm and rhyme and retell stories.
Northern Ireland	Language and literacy	KS F	• Listen to, read and retell a range of rhymes.
Republic of Ireland	English	Infants	• Listen and respond to nursery rhymes; e.g. retell a story in sequence.
Scotland	English	Level A	• Read aloud with a clear purpose.
Wales	English	KS 1	• Read material with rhyme and rhythm.

Ordering

1 Cut along the dotted lines.

2 Glue them in order at the bottom.

Leave them alone

bringing their tails behind them.

has lost her sheep

Little Bo Peep

and doesn't know where to find them.

and they will come home

3 Colour the picture.

Learning areas
English (Reading) Maths (Space)

Objectives

- Reads and understands text.
- Understands the meaning of positional words.

Resources

- cards with 'next to', 'on', 'behind', 'in' and 'in front of' written in large print
- the poem *Traffic lights* displayed in the room

TRAFFIC LIGHTS

'Stop' said the red light,
'Go' said the green,
'Be careful' said the amber,
Twinkling in between.

Lesson plan and organisation

- This activity may be done as two separate lessons.
- Worksheet may be enlarged to A3 size.
- Select hand signals for 'stop', 'go' and 'be careful'. Read the poem together, incorporating the hand signals.
- Discuss the rules in the *Traffic lights* poem and consider why traffic signals are needed.
- Read the cards and give pupils instructions to follow around the classroom; e.g. Hold up the 'next to' card and say, 'Stand next to your chair'.
- Read through the instructions for each activity before the pupils start. Ensure all pupils complete one instruction before moving onto the next.

Additional activities

- Play the game, 'Where is it?' using the positional cards and classroom objects. Pupils take turns to place an object while others choose which card correctly states where it is.
- Pupils draw and colour individual objects which may be placed within a large frame, attached using Blu-tack®. Pictures and cards may be stored next to the frame. Pupils may now play 'Where is it?' in pairs.
- Discuss rules other than traffic rules.

Answers

Teacher check

Curriculum links

Country	Subject	Level	Objectives
England	English	KS 1	• Develop contextual understanding and focus on meaning derived from text.
Northern Ireland	Language and literacy	KS F	• Read a variety of texts.
Republic of Ireland	English	Infants	• Engage in shared reading activities.
Scotland	English	Level A	• Read simple information.
Wales	English	KS 1	• Develop contextual understanding and focus on meaning derived from text.

Read and do

1 (a) Colour her hair brown.

(b) Draw a tree next to the road.

(c) Write 'stop' on the sign and colour it red.

(d) Draw a doll in the bike tray.

(e) Draw a rock behind the front wheel.

(f) Draw a blue hat on her head.

2

(a) Draw an apple next to the boy.

(b) Colour the dog's hair orange.

(c) Draw a hat on the boy.

(d) Colour the boy's shirt green.

(e) Draw a collar on the dog.

(f) Draw a cat in front of the dog.

Sounds – 1

Learning area
English (Reading and spelling)

Objectives
- Recognises initial letter sounds.
- Reads and understands text.

Resources
- pictures, posters, poems, stories and books about the animals illustrated on the worksheet (optional)
- *My dog*, a poem by Marchette Chute

Lesson plan and organisation
- Recite the *My dog* poem with actions for different shapes and sizes.
- Using animals not on the worksheet, work through some examples of each activity.
- Read the words for Question 3 with the pupils first. Explain that the adjective describes the noun or naming word. Discuss how the pupils will show 'hot'.

Additional activities
- Pupils make up their own animal phrases using adjectives; e.g. a green frog, a clever cat, a wiggly worm.
- Pupils may perform a role-play, taking on the character of their animal.

Answers
1. dog, frog, cow, bear
2. cat, fish, bug, bird
3. Teacher check

Curriculum links

Country	Subject	Level	Objectives
England	English	KS 1	• Use knowledge of sound-symbol relationships.
Northern Ireland	Language and literacy	KS F	• Explore features of written language; e.g. the beginning of words.
Republic of Ireland	English	Infants	• Learn to isolate the beginning sound of a word.
Scotland	English	Level A	• Develop an interest in how words sound.
Wales	English	KS 1	• Identify initial sounds in words.

Sounds – 1

1 Circle the animal beginning with ...

d				
f				
c				
b				

2 Write the beginning sound.

_____at   _____ish

_____ug   _____ird

3 Draw ...

| a hot sun | a fat man | a big dog |

Sounds – 2

Learning area	
Learning area English (Spelling)	**Objectives** • Recognises rhyming sounds. • Completes a word by writing the missing vowel sound.

Resources

- *I'm a little teapot* poem:

  I'm a little teapot, short and stout.
  Here's my handle, here's my spout.
  When I see the teacups, hear me shout,
  'Tip me up and pour me out!'

- pairs of objects or pictures with rhyming names; e.g. fork/cork, pen/hen, house/mouse

- *Whisky frisky* poem in large print for all to see (optional)

  Whisky Frisky, hippity-hop,
  Up he goes to the tree top.
  Whirly, twirly round and round,
  Down he scampers to the ground.
  Furly, curly what a tail!
  Tall as a feather, broad as a sail.
  Where's his supper? In the shell.
  Snappy, cracky out it fell!

  Anonymous

Lesson plan and organisation

- Read *Whisky frisky* together, using hands and arms to suggest a squirrel's movements.
- Discuss rhyming words, asking pupils to find them in the poem. Write them on the board.
- Repeat with the *I'm a little teapot* poem.
- Look at objects or pictures with rhyming names. Ask pupils to match the rhyming pairs.
- Work through Question 1 of the sheet orally, emphasising the sounds at the end which rhyme.
- Work through Question 2 orally, reading the names and choosing the correct vowel sound, for pupils to write.
- Pupils colour the worksheet.

Additional activities

- Make a chart of rhyming words suggested by the pupils. From magazines, pupils cut out pictures to illustrate the words.
- Play some oral language games using rhyming sounds; e.g. pupils make up two rhyming sentences:
  'I am a dog. I sit on a log.'; 'I am a cat. I wear a big hat.'; 'I am a mouse. I live in a house' or 'I spy with my little eye, a word that rhymes with ...'.
- Say together well-known rhymes, clapping the rhyming words.

Answers

1. hat, fan, tap, tin, sock
2. fish, bug, cat, hen, dog

Curriculum links

Country	Subject	Level	Objectives
England	English	KS 1	• Link sound and letter patterns, exploring rhyme.
Northern Ireland	Language and literacy	KS F	• Explore features of written language; e.g. the end of words.
Republic of Ireland	English	Infants	• Learn to isolate the part of a word which allows it to rhyme with another word.
Scotland	English	Level A	• Develop an interest in how words sound and the patterns within them.
Wales	English	KS 1	• Recognise rhyme and relate this to patterns in letters.

1 Write the word that rhymes.

mat

 h _ _

man

 f _ _ _

cap

 t _ _ _

pin

 t _ _ _

clock

 s _ _ _ _

2 Write the missing sound.

a e i o u

f _ _ sh

b _ _ g

c _ _ t

h _ _ n

d _ _ g

Single sounds – 't'

E

Learning area English (Reading and spelling)	**Objective** • Recognises words with 't' as an initial letter sound.

Resources
- collection of objects and pictures of objects beginning with 't'
- three toys: teddy bear, turtle and tiger

Lesson plan and organisation
- Introduce the sound 't' with a poem with 't' in it; for example, *Teddy bear, teddy bear*.
- Look at the collection of resources, naming each and emphasising the 't' sound at the beginning. Write each word on the board. Underline the letter 't'.
- Look around the classroom for objects beginning with 't'. Say the name and write the word on the board.
- Bring out each toy, one at a time, saying the name and writing the word on the board.
- Read each instruction, and any unknown words, for pupils to complete the worksheet.

Additional activities
- Make up alliterative phrases with the letter 't'; e.g. ten tiny teddies, two tired tigers.
- Learn other poems about 'two'; for example, *Two fat gentlemen* and *Two little dicky birds*.
- Repeat the whole procedure with other initial letter sounds. Make up similar worksheets.

Answers
1. teddy, turtle, tiger
2. (a) ten tiny teddies   (b) two tired tigers

Curriculum links

Country	Subject	Level	Objectives
England	English	KS 1	• Use knowledge of sound-symbol relationships.
Northern Ireland	Language and literacy	KS F	• Explore features of written language; e.g. the beginning of words.
Republic of Ireland	English	Infants	• Learn to isolate the beginning sound of a word.
Scotland	English	Level A	• Develop an interest in how words sound.
Wales	English	KS 1	• Identify initial sounds in words.

1 Write the missing 't'.

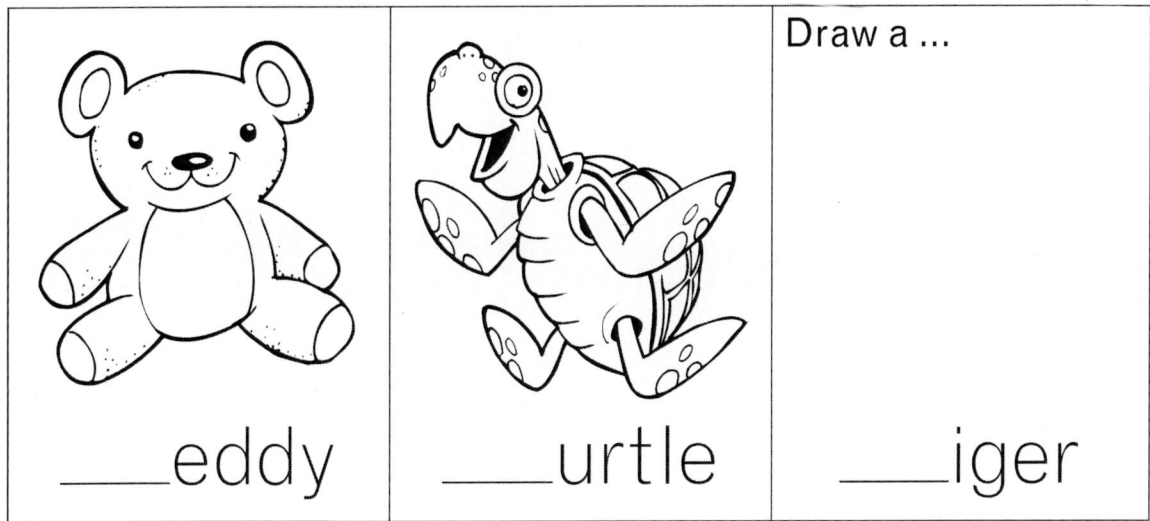

Draw a ...

___eddy   ___urtle   ___iger

2 Write the missing 't' and draw a picture.

(a)

___en   ___iny   ___eddies

(b)

___wo   ___ired   ___igers

My cat

Learning area
English (Writing)

Objectives
* Describes features of cats.
* Writes about a pet cat.

Resources
* a poem or rhyme with a cat as a central character; for example *Who is that?* by Barbara Ireson and Christopher Rowe
* cat stories; e.g. *Puss in boots*, *Slinky Malinki* and *Scarface Claw* by Lynley Dodd

Lesson plan and organisation
* Read and say some cat poems and rhymes or read a story about cats to the pupils.
* Discuss the personalities and characters of these fictional animals. Write the words on the board.
* Discuss pupils' pet cats. Pupils who do not have a pet may think of someone else's cat; e.g. Grandma, friend, cousin. Alternatively, they may choose to describe a cat they would like to own. Write words on the board describing how cats look, move, behave and what they do.
* Write sentence starters on the board; e.g. My cat loves ..., When my cat goes out ..., Sometimes, my cat ... .
* Pupils write about their cats, with aid from adult helpers as required.

Additional activities
* View scenes from the *Aristocats* film.
* Role-play cats from poems and rhymes.
* Pupils include a photograph or drawn picture of a cat with their writing.
* Make a chain of cat stories pupils have read.
* Invite a child or parent to bring a cat for a visit.

Answers
Teacher check

Curriculum links

Country	Subject	Level	Objectives
England	English	KS 1	• Use a range of writing forms.
Northern Ireland	Language and literacy	KS F	• See themselves as 'writers' and use a range of writing forms.
Republic of Ireland	English	Infants	• Write frequently.
Scotland	English	Level A	• Produce functional and personal writing.
Wales	English	KS 1	• Write in response to a variety of stimuli and in a range of forms.

My cat

by _____

The relief teacher toolkit

<table>
<tr><td>**Learning area**
English
(Writing)</td><td>**Objectives**
• Writes a story following a simple plan.
• Considers the range of transport used for different purposes.</td></tr>
</table>

Resources

• big book *Around and about* by Amanda Graham and Leanne Argent – ERA Publications or any big book on the theme of transport

Lesson plan and organisation

• Use *Around and about* as a springboard for discussion on travel. Discuss different modes of transport for different purposes.

• Discuss journeys pupils have made, detailing type of transport, who, where, when and why.

• Make a list of sentence starters; e.g. Last week; On Thursday evening; During the holidays; Dad drove us to ...; We visited ... .

• List words pupils will need for their stories.

• Pupils write and illustrate their stories using the chart as a plan.

Additional activities

• Pupils make a montage using a collection of transport pictures cut from magazines.

• Collect stories in a large scrapbook and paste the montage on to the cover. Display.

• Tape pupils reading their stories.

• Find and display books about different modes of transport.

• Survey and graph forms of transport used by pupils.

Answers

Teacher check

Curriculum links

Country	Subject	Level	Objectives
England	English	KS 1	• Use a range of writing forms.
Northern Ireland	Language and literacy	KS F	• See themselves as 'writers' and use a range of writing forms.
Republic of Ireland	English	Infants	• Write stories.
Scotland	English	Level A	• Produce imaginative writing.
Wales	English	KS 1	• Write in response to a variety of stimuli and in a range of forms.

My trip

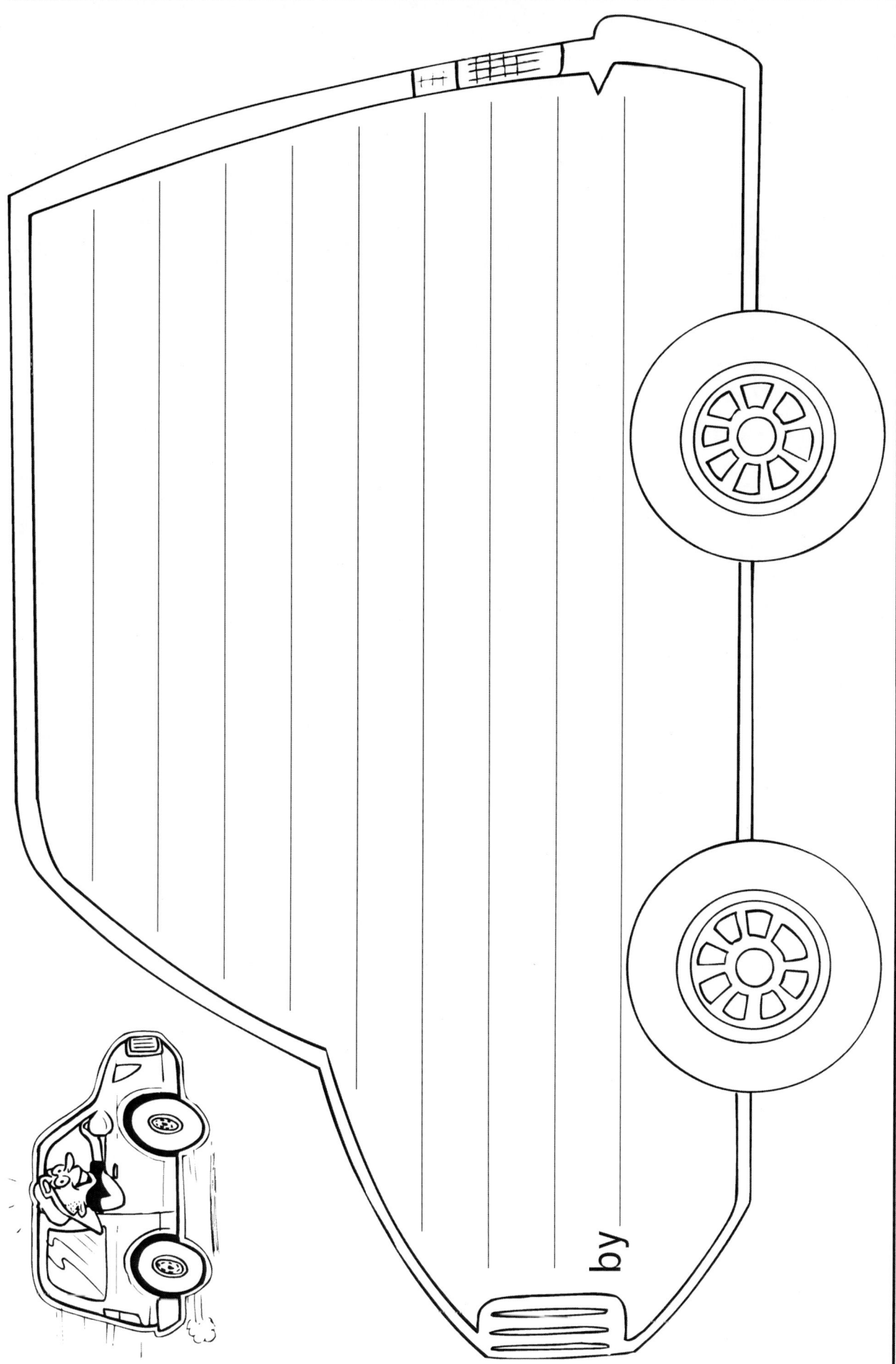

by

The relief teacher toolkit

<table>
<tr><td rowspan="2">Learning area
English
(Writing)</td><td>Objectives</td></tr>
<tr><td>
• Considers an item of interest for news.

• Discusses its key features.

• Writes an account of the news.
</td></tr>
</table>

Resources

• pupils bring in items to illustrate their news

Lesson plan and organisation

• Write the headings from the sheet on the board.

• Explain that these headings will help pupils to organise the way they present their news. Give some examples of your news, following these headings. Give some pupils the opportunity to do the same.

• In pairs, pupils discuss their news.

• Pupils write and illustrate their news on the planning sheets. Adult assistance may be needed for some words.

Additional activities

• Pupils use the sheet as a plan to write their news as a story.

• Pupils share news items they have seen and heard on television and radio.

• Make a Monday to Friday diary in which pupils can record news items they have heard. These may be read out at the end of each day.

• Pupils can present their stories as a news item on television.

Answers

Teacher check

Curriculum links

Country	Subject	Level	Objectives
England	English	KS 1	• Use a range of writing forms.
Northern Ireland	Language and literacy	KS F	• See themselves as 'writers' and use a range of writing forms.
Republic of Ireland	English	Infants	• Write about everyday experiences and feelings.
Scotland	English	Level A	• Produce personal writing.
Wales	English	KS 1	• Write in response to a variety of stimuli and in a range of forms.

My news

Day: _____

Who is your news about?

_____

Tell what happened:

_____

_____

_____

_____

_____

How did you feel?

_____

_____

_____

_____

_____

Draw what happened.

The relief teacher toolkit

Recount

Learning area	Objectives
English (Writing)	• Identifies key events in a story. • Places events in correct sequence.

Resources

• selection of well-known short stories and rhymes

Lesson plan and organisation

• Write the first four headings from the sheet across the top of the board. Explain to the pupils that these will be used to recount the story. Read a well-known story such as *The three little pigs*. Encourage the pupils to make suggestions to put under each heading on the board.

• Discuss stories the pupils have personally experienced and ask them to recount them orally, following the same headings.

• Explain that the final heading on the sheet gives them an opportunity to express their opinion of the story.

• Pupils may complete a draft copy of their recount before copying onto the worksheet.

• Pupils choose a personal experience to recount on the sheet. It may help some pupils to illustrate their recounts before they write them. These may be used as prompts for writing.

Additional activities

• Pupils use recounts to deliver an oral report.

• Pupils choose a short story to illustrate as a sequence of pictures highlighting the main events.

Answers

Teacher check

Curriculum links

Country	Subject	Level	Objectives
England	English	KS 1	• Use a range of writing forms.
Northern Ireland	Language and literacy	KS F	• See themselves as 'writers' and use a range of writing forms.
Republic of Ireland	English	Infants	• Hear a variety of stories and write about them.
Scotland	English	Level A	• Produce imaginative writing.
Wales	English	KS 1	• Write in response to a variety of stimuli and in a range of forms.

Recount

Event: _____

Where did it take place?

_____

What happened?

_____

_____

_____

_____

_____

_____

_____

_____

_____

How did it end?

_____

_____

_____

What do you think?

_____

_____

Nursery rhyme writing

<table>
<tr><td>Learning area
English
(Handwriting)</td><td>Objectives
• Practises a smooth handwriting rhythm.
• Demonstrates motor skills for writing.</td></tr>
</table>

Resources

• nursery rhyme books with *Humpty Dumpty* and *Jack and Jill* (optional)

• large copy of each of these rhymes for display

Lesson plan and organisation

• This activity may be done as two separate lessons.

• On the board, show pupils how they will draw the eight ovals, starting at the side and working anticlockwise in one smooth movement. As they recite the rhyme, they will draw each oval as indicated on the sheet. Pupils illustrate the rhyme, drawing in each oval. Teachers may demonstrate simple figures for pupils to copy.

• Show the pupils how to draw the eight peaks, starting at the bottom on the left-hand side. As the rhyme is recited, they draw each peak as indicated on the sheet. Pupils may create patterns in each triangle.

• Pupils colour the titles.

Additional activities

• Pupils make *Humpty Dumpty* characters using boiled eggs for the body, adding facial features with marker pens.

• Print lines from three nursery rhymes onto card. Mix them up and place them face down. In groups of three, each pupil is given a rhyme to collect. They take turns choosing a card. The winner is the first to collect their complete rhyme.

• Pupils 'take their pencils for a walk'. Holding the pencil firmly but lightly, pupils draw a smooth, random pattern over a blank page, crossing lines to make shapes and finally taking the pencil off the page at the starting point. Pupils colour the resulting shapes.

Answers

Teacher check

Curriculum links

Country	Subject	Level	Objectives
England	English	KS 1	• Hold a pencil comfortably in order to develop a legible handwriting style.
Northern Ireland	Language and literacy	KS F	• Develop physical and manipulative skills.
Republic of Ireland	English	Infants	• Write and draw shapes and develop a satisfactory grip of writing implements.
Scotland	English	Level A	• Draw to develop hand-eye coordination.
Wales	English	KS 1	• Hold a pencil comfortably in order to develop a legible handwriting style.

Humpty Dumpty

Humpty Dumpty	sat on the wall	Humpty Dumpty	had a great fall.

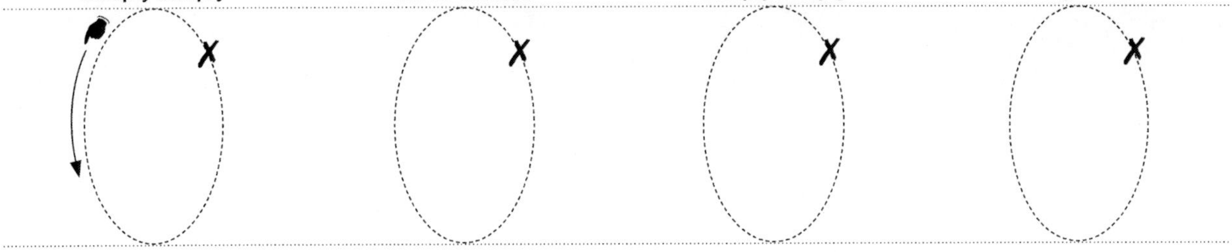

All the king's horses	and all the king's men	Couldn't put Humpty	together again.

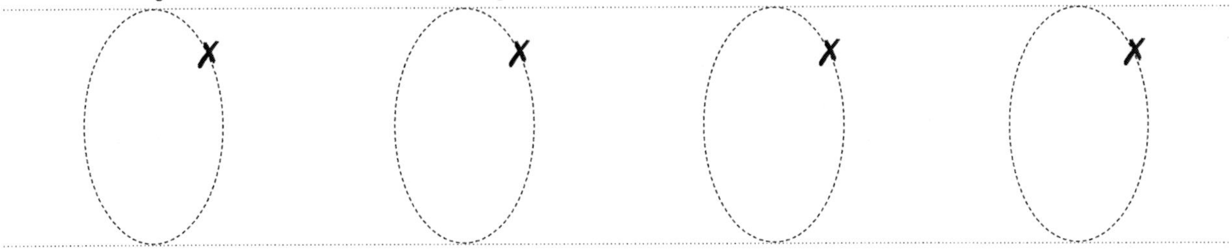

Jack and Jill

Jack and Jill	went up the hill	to fetch a pail	of water.

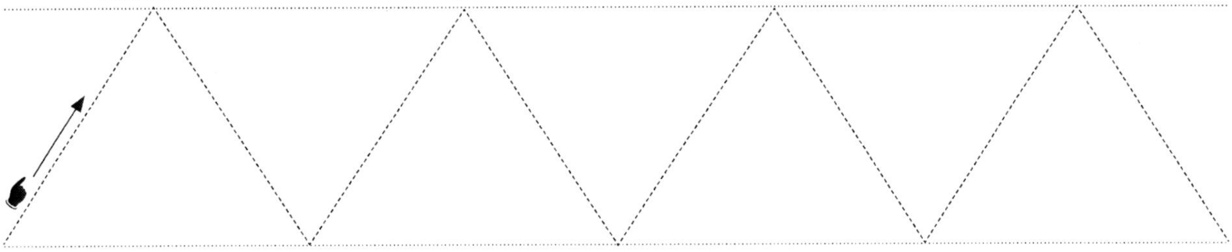

Jack fell down	and broke his crown	and Jill came tumbling	after.

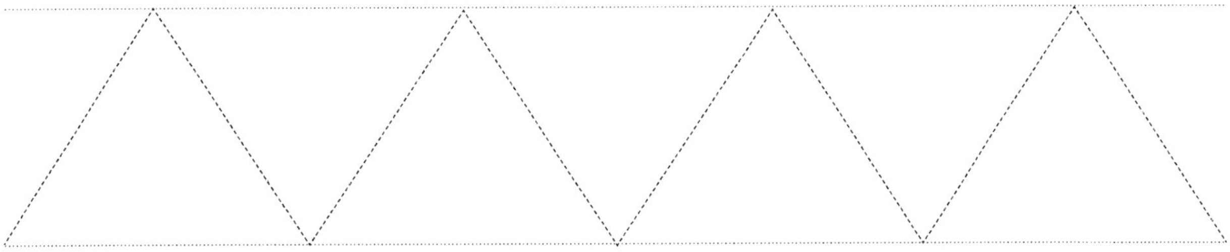

Learning area	Objective
English (Handwriting)	• Uses written symbols to convey a message.

Resources

• nursery rhyme books with *This little piggy*, *Twinkle, twinkle little star* and *Baa baa black sheep* (optional)

• large copy of each rhyme for display

Lesson plan and organisation

• Recite the first rhyme with the class, pointing to the lines of the rhyme so the pupils can see the words.

• Demonstrate spiral patterns in the air as you say the rhyme. Clearly show that each spiral matches a line of the rhyme.

This little piggy

 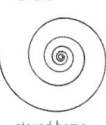 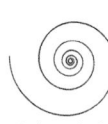  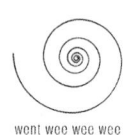 

went to market   stayed home   had roast beef   had none   went wee wee wee   children draw pigs later

• Pupils practise making spirals in the air and on scrap paper before drawing them on the worksheet. Demonstrate how the spirals can be transformed into simple pictures of pigs by the addition of a few lines.

• Repeat the activity with the other two rhymes, replacing the spiral with a ✳ for *Twinkle, twinkle little star*, then a ◯ for *Baa baa black sheep*.

Additional activities

• Pupils use symbols and patterns to represent things in other rhymes. Ask classmates to identify the rhyme. Complete symbols on art paper and decorate using wax resist techniques etc. to use for book covers or wrapping paper.

• Using available craft resources, make a large class display of a chosen rhyme.

• Use cotton wool to make sheep shapes; cardboard shapes and glitter to create stars etc.

Answers

Teacher check

Curriculum links

Country	Subject	Level	Objectives
England	English	KS 1	• Hold a pencil comfortably in order to develop a legible handwriting style.
Northern Ireland	Language and literacy	KS F	• Develop physical and manipulative skills.
Republic of Ireland	English	Infants	• Write and draw shapes and develop a satisfactory grip of writing implements.
Scotland	English	Level A	• Draw to develop hand-eye coordination.
Wales	English	KS 1	• Hold a pencil comfortably in order to develop a legible handwriting style.

This little piggy

Twinkle, twinkle little star

Baa baa black sheep

Numbers

Learning area Mathematics (Number)	**Objectives** • Identifies an object in a given position (ordinal numbers). • Counts and draws a specific number of objects.

Resources

- small toys; e.g. animals, cars, plastic food, dolls furniture (at least 10)

- counting materials; e.g. blocks, counters

- large copy of *1 2 3 4 5* rhyme

  Six verses:
  1 – thumbs
  2 – pointers
  3 – tall men
  4 – ring men
  5 – small men
  6 – all men.

  One, two, three, four, five,
  My little *thumbs* are all alive.
  First wag this way, then wag that,
  My little *thumbs*, what are you at?

Lesson plan and organisation

- This activity is ideally suited to small-group work with the teacher or assistant.

- Recite the *1 2 3 4 5* action rhyme with the pupils.

- **Question 1:** Line up the toys. Ask questions relating to number order; e.g. 'Which toy is 5th?', 'In which place is the cat?' Pupils complete Question 1.

- **Question 2:** Using counting materials, display different amounts of material and ask pupils to count them. They may need to move each counter aside as it is counted. On the worksheet, they may wish to put a cross on each object as they count it, or number each.

- **Question 3:** Practise first, giving pupils a number of objects to count out in blocks or counters. Pupils then draw their own objects.

Additional activities

- Pupils work in pairs, taking turns to ask each other to count out a given number of objects or the position of a particular object in a row.

- Pupils view the ordinal words and abbreviations to use for future reference.

Answers

1. Teacher check

2. (a) 11   (b) 9   (c) 8   (d) 7

3. Teacher check

Curriculum links

Country	Subject	Level	Objectives
England	Maths	KS 1	• Count objects reliably and use correct vocabulary to order numbers.
Northern Ireland	Maths and numeracy	KS F	• Count objects and explore ordinal number.
Republic of Ireland	Maths	Infants	• Count objects in a set and use the language of ordinal number.
Scotland	Maths	Level A	• Count and order numbers.
Wales	Maths	KS 1	• Count objects reliably.

Numbers

1 Circle

4th	
2nd	
3rd	
6th	

2 Count

(a)

(b)

(c)

(d)

3 Draw

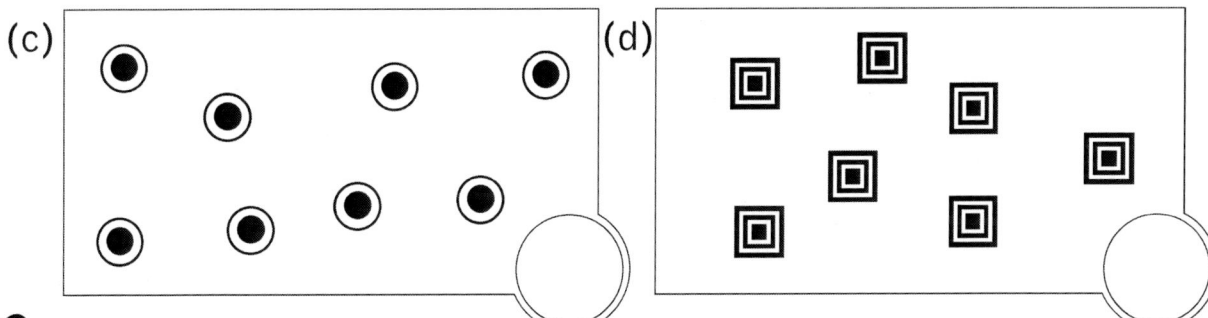

8

6

The relief teacher toolkit

How many?

Learning area Mathematics (Number)	Objectives • Draws objects to solve addition problems. • Understands different ways of solving subtraction problems.

Resources

- a repertoire of appropriate rhymes; for example:

  Takeaway rhymes:

  Ten fat sausages, counting down in twos;

  Ten fat sausages frying in a pan,
  One went pop and another went bang!
  Eight fat sausages ... etc.

  Five little ducks, counting down in ones;

  Five little ducks went out one day,
  Over the hills and far away.
  Mother duck said,
  'Quack! Quack! Quack! Quack!'
  But only four little ducks came back ... etc.

- number rhyme books include:
  Nonsense counting rhymes by Kaye Umansky and Chris Fisher
  One, two, skip a few! First number rhymes by Barefoot books

Lesson plan and organisation

- Recite finger rhymes, explaining how the numbers get smaller with each subtraction.
- Use a number–related big book to introduce a selection of simple number activities.
- Using the pupils and objects around the classroom, orally present a range of number activities similar to those on the worksheet. Write some examples on the board.
- As pupils complete the sheet, encourage them to mark the pictures as they count them to avoid errors.

Additional activities

- Pupils work in pairs, taking turns to pose their own questions orally and pictorially.
- Present research information as a block graph and ask number questions relating to it; for example, the months of pupils' birthdays: How many pupils were born in March? How many more were born in April than in July?
- Ask pupils to help with classroom organisation where knowledge of numbers is required; e.g. How many paint pots are needed for this group? How many bats and balls are needed for that group?

Answers

1. (a) 3   (b) 4
2. (a) 10   (b) 5
3. (a) 8   (b) 5
4. (a) 10   (b) 5   (c) 5

Curriculum links

Country	Subject	Level	Objectives
England	Maths	KS 1	• Know addition and subtraction facts and solve whole number problems.
Northern Ireland	Maths and numeracy	KS F	• Carry out simple mental calculations.
Republic of Ireland	Maths	Infants	• Solve simple oral and pictorial problems.
Scotland	Maths	Level A	• Add and subtract.
Wales	Maths	KS 1	• Understand addition and subtraction and use them to solve problems with whole numbers.

The relief teacher toolkit   Prim-Ed Publishing   www.prim-ed.com

How many?

1 Count and draw.

(a) How many more to make 6? ☐

(b) How many more to make 8? ☐

2

(a) How many plants altogether? ☐
Five plants die. Cross them out.

(b) How many are still alive? ☐

3

(a) How many bunnies altogether? ☐
Three bunnies hop away. Cross them out.

(b) How many are left? ☐

4

(a) How many cows? ☐

(b) How many horses? ☐

(c) How many more cows than horses are there? ☐

This old man

Learning area
Mathematics (Number)

Objectives

• Recognises numbers from 1 to 10 in numeral and word form.

• Correctly matches numeral and word for numbers 1 to 10.

Resources

• large copy of *This old man* rhyme:

This old man, he played one,
He played knick knack on my drum,
With a knick knack paddy whack, give a dog a bone,
This old man came rolling home.

two – shoe, three – knee, four – door, five – hive, six – sticks,
seven – up in Heaven, eight – gate, nine – spine, ten – pen

• the number words from one to ten written on the board, but not in order

Lesson plan and organisation

• Sing the rhyme together, showing the numbers on fingers.

• Read the word numerals from the board as the pupils trace them on the sheets. Encourage them to copy them correctly. Pupils match the numbers with the correct pictures as the rhyme is sung again.

Additional activities

• Pupils find other objects to rhyme with the numbers.

• Make a list of number rhymes.

Answers

1 = drum, 2 = shoe, 3 = knee, 4 = door, 5 = hive, 6 = sticks, 7 = Heaven, 8 = gate, 9 = spine, 10 = pen

Curriculum links

Country	Subject	Level	Objectives
England	Maths	KS 1	• Count, read and write numbers.
Northern Ireland	Maths and numeracy	KS F	• Recognise numerals up to 10 and count in the context of number rhymes.
Republic of Ireland	Maths	Infants	• Count, read and write numbers; e.g. use number rhymes.
Scotland	Maths	Level A	• Count, read and write numbers.
Wales	Maths	KS 1	• Count, read and write numbers.

This old man

Trace the number word and match the picture to the correct number.

1 →	one	●		●	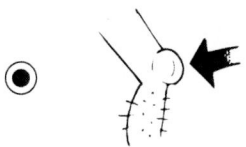
2 →	two	●		●	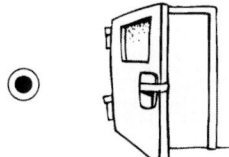
3 →	three	●		●	
4 →	four	●		●	
5 →	five	●		●	
6 →	six	●		●	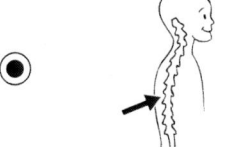
7 →	seven	●		●	
8 →	eight	●		●	
9 →	nine	●		●	
10 →	ten	●		●	

It's time!

Learning area	Objectives
Mathematics (Measurement)	• Sequences daily events. • Indicates 'o'clock' using an analogue clock.

Resources

- large clock with freely moving hour and minute hands
- today's date written on the board; e.g. Monday 1 June
- library resources: poems about the time of day, days of the week, months and seasons of the year (optional)
- *What time is it?* by Barbara Ireson and Christopher Rowe

Lesson plan and organisation

- Discuss the concept of time in terms of what is already familiar; e.g. today's date, time of day, before/after break, school term, the season.
- Revise telling the time, o'clock only. Ask time questions:
  'At what time do you ...?' eat breakfast, go to school, have lunch, go home, exercise, have a bath, go to bed.
  Show times by moving the hour hand on the clock.
- In pairs or groups, pupils discuss their preferred time of day and write a sentence to explain why.

- Read *What time is it?* poem.
- Pupils write today's date on the worksheet as directed. Ask pupils what they like to do at the different times of day shown on the worksheet. Discuss and write appropriate times for each segment of the circle. Pupils draw the shorter (hour) hand pointing to appropriate number on the clock face and write the time. Pupils draw pictures to illustrate what they like to do at each time.

Additional activities

- Pupils write sentences to indicate what they do at different times of the day.
- Pupils complete a simple weekly class timetable, including activities which require them to leave their room; e.g. physical education, music. Pupils note the time of these activities.
- Pupils complete a 'Seasons wheel', including major events which occur in particular seasons; e.g. Christmas.

Answers

Teacher check

Curriculum links

Country	Subject	Level	Objectives
England	Maths	KS 1	• Put familiar events in chronological order and use standard units of time.
Northern Ireland	Maths and numeracy	KS F	• Sequence familiar events and talk about significant times on the clock.
Republic of Ireland	Maths	Infants	• Sequence daily events and read time in one-hour intervals.
Scotland	Maths	Level A	• Place events in time sequence and tell the time in whole hours using analogue displays.
Wales	Maths	KS 1	• Order events in time and begin to use standard units of time.

The relief teacher toolkit   Prim-Ed Publishing   www.prim-ed.com

It's time!

1 Complete the sentences.

Today is _____.

It is the _____ day of _____.

2 Draw to show what you will do at these times:

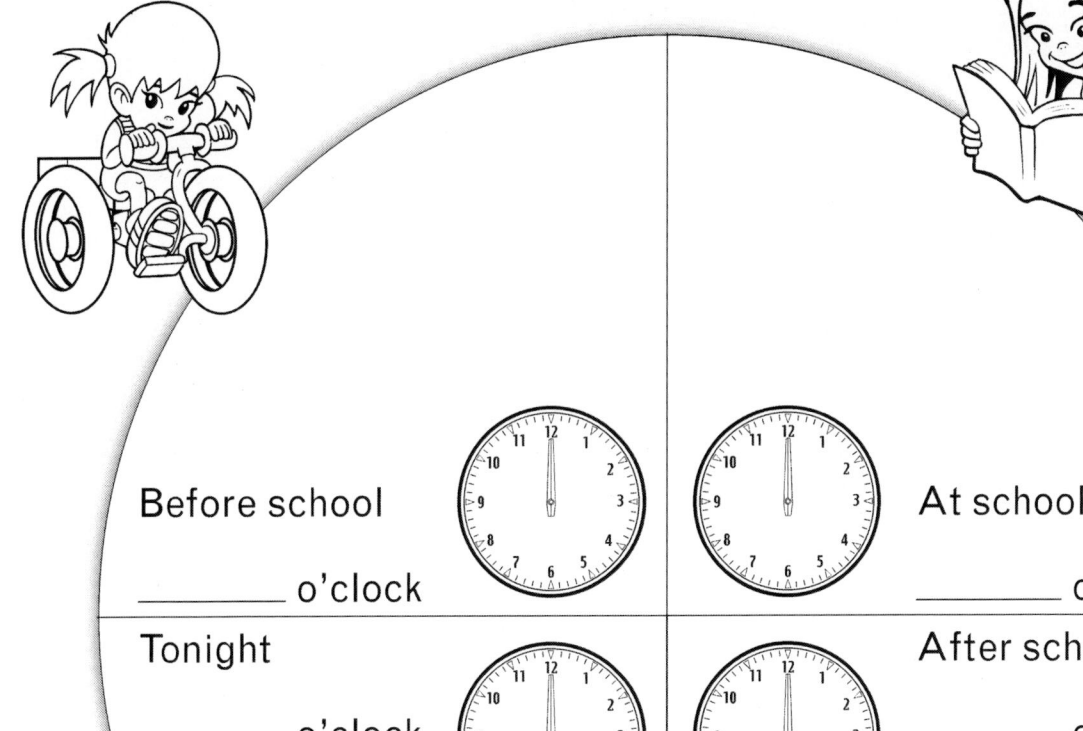

Before school

_____ o'clock

At school

_____ o'clock

Tonight

_____ o'clock

After school

_____ o'clock

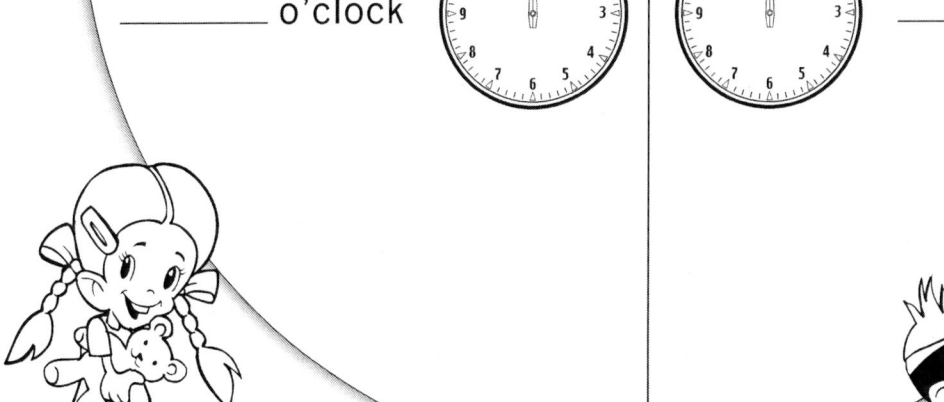

3 Complete the sentence.

The time of day I like best is _____

because _____

_____

Circles, squares and triangles

Learning area
Mathematics (Shape and data)

Objectives

• Differentiates between 2-D shapes.

• Records data about 2-D shapes on a bar chart.

• Recognises 2-D shapes in everyday objects.

Resources

• plastic squares, circles and triangles of different sizes

Lesson plan and organisation

• Display a square and discuss its features; i.e. number of sides, corners and lengths of sides. Take another square and ask what shape it is. Compare with first square. It may be bigger or smaller but it is still a square. Look around the room for any objects with a square face.

• Repeat procedure with circles and then with triangles.

• Using a different colour for each, pupils colour, count and record the number of each shape on the worksheet.

• Pupils choose objects from around the class to complete Questions 6 and 7. Teachers may list the names of appropriate objects on the board for pupils to choose and copy.

Additional activities

• Cut out a selection of squares, circles and triangles for the pupils to use to make 'shape figures', which are held together with string.

• Pupils make patterns using 2-D shapes.

Answers

1. Teacher check
2. squares = 7, circles = 4, triangles = 8
3. 19
4. triangles
5. circles
6–7. Teacher check

Curriculum links

Country	Subject	Level	Objectives
England	Maths	KS 1	• Name common 2-D shapes and use simple charts to classify information.
Northern Ireland	Maths and numeracy	KS F	• Name common 2-D shapes and investigate ways of representing data; e.g. block graphs.
Republic of Ireland	Maths	Infants	• Name 2-D shapes and represent data.
Scotland	Maths	Level A/B	• Name squares, triangles and circles and display data on a bar graph.
Wales	Maths	KS 1	• Recognise squares, circles and triangles and record data on graphs.

1 Choose a colour for each shape and colour them.

2 Count each shape and colour the correct number on the graph.

9			
8			
7			
6			
5			
4			
3			
2			
1			
	squares	circles	triangles

squares = _____

circles = _____

triangles = _____

3 How many shapes are there? _____

4 Which shape had the most? _____

5 Which shape had the least? _____

6 Name and draw something shaped like a circle.

_____

7 Name and draw something shaped like a triangle.

_____

Animal match

Learning area	Objectives
Science	• Recognises differences and similarities between animals.
	• Groups animals according to selected criteria.

Resources

• pictures and models of the creatures on the lesson sheet (optional)

• *Jump or jiggle*, a poem by Evelyn Beyer and/or other rhymes or poems about how animals move

Websites

• Find out about different animals: http://nationalzoo.si.edu/default.cfm

• All about animals: http://www.enchantedlearning.com/coloring/ http://www.twycrosszoo.com/listofanimalsatthezoo.htm

Lesson plan and organisation

• Begin the lesson in an open space where pupils can move freely.

• Say the rhymes together. Include body actions where appropriate.

• Discuss the different creatures and how they move.

• Look at the animals on the sheet. Discuss ways in which they may be grouped.

• Pupils cut out animals and place them before gluing.

Additional activities

• Prepare pictures of a wider selection of animals for the pupils to colour. Discuss how they might be grouped. Print the names of the animals on strips of paper. Pupils match the pictures and names. Label sheets of card with the name of each group. Pupils place and glue the named animals on the correct sheet of card. Display sheets. Count the number in each group.

Answers

1. Teacher check

2. fly – bird, bee, butterfly

   four legs – donkey, camel, cow

   fins – fish, shark, dolphin

   no legs/fins – worm, snail, snake

Curriculum links

Country	Subject	Level	Objectives
England	Science	KS 1	• Group living things according to observable similarities.
Northern Ireland	Science	KS F	• Identify similarities in living things.
Republic of Ireland	Science	Infants	• Sort and group living things into sets and recognise the external parts of living things.
Scotland	Science	Level A	• Sort living things into broad groups according to easily observable characteristics.
Wales	Science	KS 1	• Group living things according to observable similarities.

Animal match

1 Colour and cut out the animals.

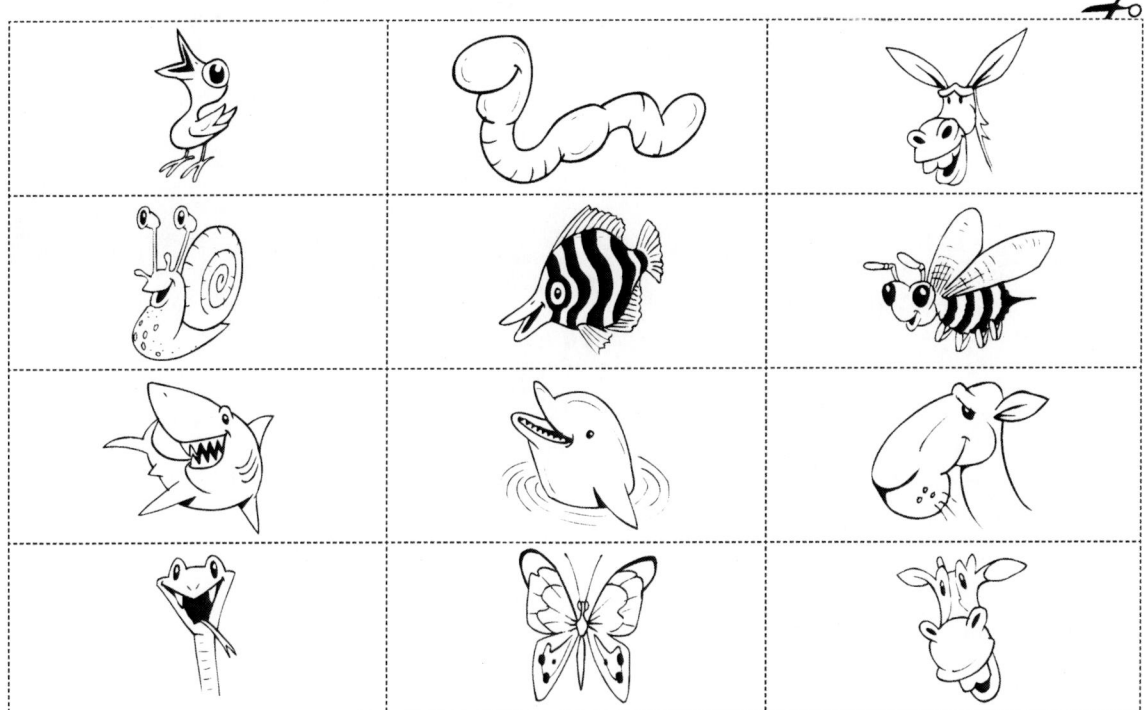

2 Glue the animals in the right box.

Animals that can fly.		
Animals with four legs.		
Animals with fins.		
Animals with no legs or fins.		

Young and adult

Learning area	Objectives
Science	• Matches young and adults of a species. • Recognises the young and adult characteristics of some animals.

Resources

- library resources showing young and adult of various animals and plants (optional)
- stories, poems, rhymes about animals changing from young to old:
  e.g. *The very hungry caterpillar* by Eric Carle, *From tadpole to frog* by Wendy Pfeffer, *The ugly duckling* (traditional), *The caterpillar* by Christina Rossetti

Lesson plan and organisation

- Look at pictures of young and adult animals. How are they different? How are they the same?
- Discuss how babies change as they grow older. What things happen along the way? Note that many animal young are smaller versions of the adult and that change is with size, maturity and skill level. Some young are a little different from their parents, particularly birds; e.g. cygnets and swans, ducklings and ducks, chicks and hens. For some creatures, notably frogs and butterflies, the change is complete. Use library resources to illustrate these changes.
- Write the words from the list on the board and read through them with the pupils, who match them with the correct picture and label.

- Pupils choose another example of young and adult to draw in the empty boxes.
- Discuss the similarities and differences between kittens and cats. Consider their habits and behaviour as well as their physical appearance and sounds. Write helpful words and phrases on the board. Pupils complete question 4.

Additional activities

- Pupils cut out pictures from magazines and make a montage of young and adult animals.
- Pupils present mini-topics on their own pets, including photographs, showing how they have changed over time.
- Pupils role-play specific animal behaviours.
- Label three sheets of card, 'Almost the same', 'A little different' and 'Very different'. Pupils find pictures of young and adult animals for each sheet. Display sheets.

Answers

1. Teacher check
2. Chick and hen, caterpillar and butterfly, rosebud and rose, tadpole and frog
3.–4. Teacher check

Curriculum links

Country	Subject	Level	Objectives
England	Science	KS 1	• Know that animals grow and that offspring grow into adults.
Northern Ireland	Science	KS F	• Recognise that animals change over time.
Republic of Ireland	Science	Infants	• Observe growth and change in living things.
Scotland	Science	Level B	• Recognise stages in the lifecycles of familiar animals.
Wales	Science	KS 1	• Know that animals grow and that offspring grow into adults.

Young and adult

1 Match the picture of the young with the adult.

2 Write the names under each picture.

hen   tadpole   rosebud   caterpillar

chick   rose   frog   butterfly

Young   ### Adult

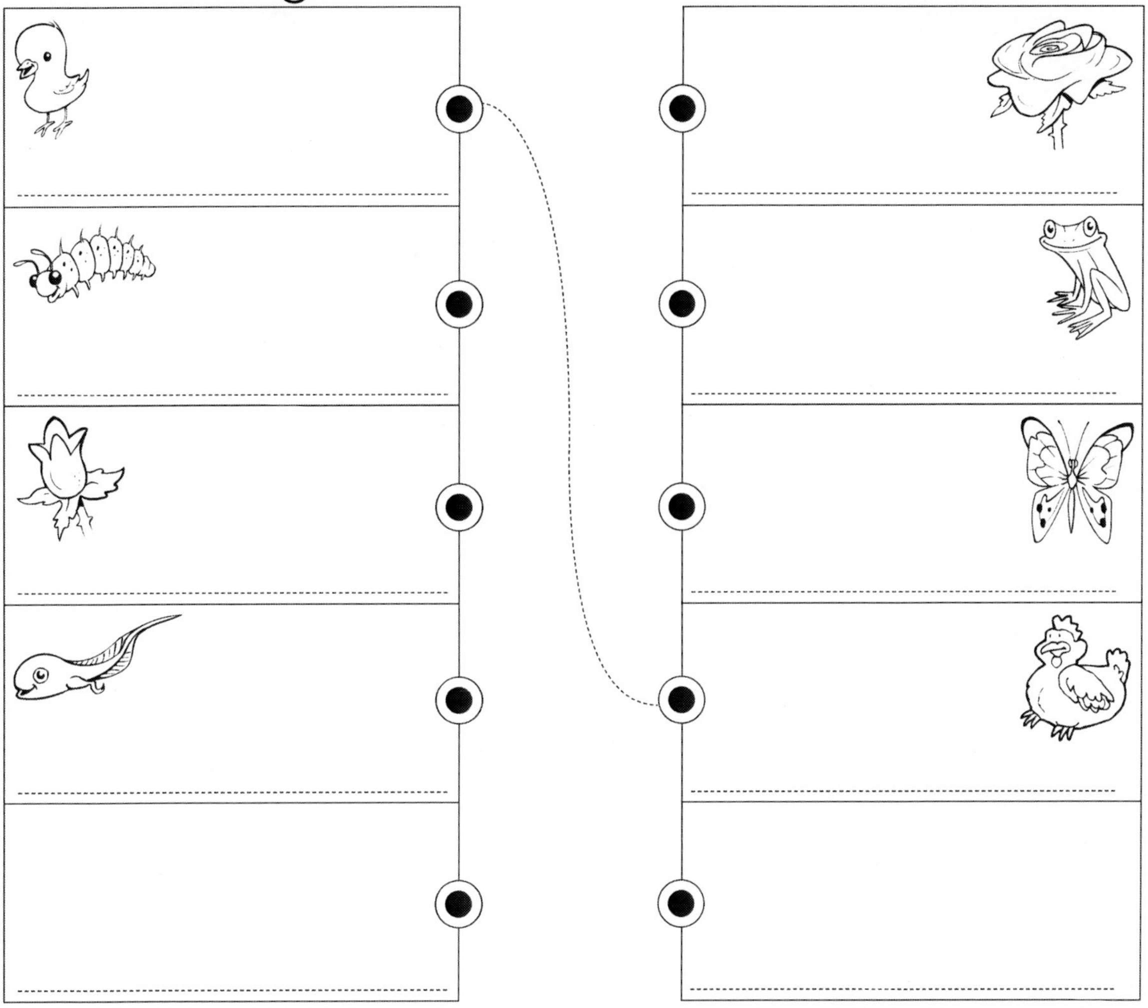

3 (a) Draw another young and adult in the blank boxes.

(b) Write their names.

4 Tell how a kitten is different from a cat.

A kitten is _____

_____.

A cat is _____

_____.

Learning area	Objectives
Science	• Understands which body parts are involved in the use of the five senses.
	• Appreciates the value of his/her senses by considering what each is used for.

Resources

- things to test each sense; e.g. fruit to taste, a bell to hear, different textured materials to feel, perfume to smell, a picture to see

- *Two little eyes*, a poem by Barbara Ireson and Christopher Rowe

- magnifying glasses (optional)

Website

- Learn about the five senses: http://library.thinkquest.org/3750/?tqskip1=1

Lesson plan and organisation

- Use the poem to introduce/revise the senses. Write the keywords on the board. Play 'Simon says point to your ...' ears, eyes, mouth and nose.

- Taking each sense in turn, discuss the things we can see, hear, smell, taste or feel. Use the material brought in for pupils to use their senses. Pupils give examples of their favourite sights, sounds etc. Write keywords and phrases on the board.

- Pupils draw the correct body part for each sense.

- Pupils complete Question 2.

Additional activities

- Play 'Feely bag'. An object which the pupil cannot see, hear, taste or smell is placed in a feely bag. He/She has to use his/her sense of touch to identify it.

- Play 'Blindfold taste test'. A pupil is blindfolded and asked to sample some food, using his/her sense of taste to identify it.

- Use a magnifying glass to allow pupils to clearly see the pores and hairs of their skin.

Answers

1. taste – mouth/tongue, sight – eyes, smell – nose, hearing – ears, touch – hands/skin/fingers

2. Teacher check

Curriculum links

Country	Subject	Level	Objectives
England	Science	KS 1	• Recognise the external human body parts and know that senses enable humans to be aware of the world around them.
Northern Ireland	PD	KS F	• Explore who they are and what they can do.
Republic of Ireland	Science	Infants	• Identify parts of the human body and use all the senses to be aware of environments.
Scotland	Science	Level A/B	• Name the main external parts of the human body and give examples of how the senses are used to detect information.
Wales	Science	KS 1	• Name the main external parts of the human body and know that senses enable humans to be aware of the world around them.

The five senses

1 Draw the part of the body we use for each sense.

taste

sight

hearing

smell

touch

2 Complete each sentence, saying what you use each sense for.

(a) I use my eyes to see _____.

(b) I use my nose to smell _____.

(c) I use my mouth to taste _____.

(d) I use my skin to touch _____.

(e) I use my ears to hear _____.

About your teeth

Learning area
Health

Objectives
- Appreciates the need for good oral hygiene.
- Learns which foods to choose and which to avoid for better oral health.

Resources
- collection of dental care products
- magazines with dental product advertising
- small make-up mirrors

Websites
- All about teeth: www.healthyteeth.org/index.html

Lesson plan and organisation
- Introduce the lesson with a story or a poem; for example, *Dear tooth fairy* (Walker Books), *Titus's troublesome tooth* (Little Tiger Press) and *Dave and the tooth fairy* (Tamarind).

- Discuss dental hygiene and what pupils should be doing to care for their teeth. Explain in simple terms the damage caused by poor dental hygiene. Consider the benefits of eating raw fruit and vegetables, dairy products and drinking water, and the problems caused by having food and drink with a high sugar content. Write keywords and phrases on the board.

- Discuss how first teeth fall out naturally and how second teeth grow. Ask pupils how many have already lost some teeth. Using the mirrors, ask them to try to count their teeth. (Clean hands before and after!) Explain that looking after first teeth is very important, even though they will be falling out!

- Pupils complete the worksheet.

Additional activities
- Read fiction and nonfiction related to the care of teeth.

- Make a toothbrush from cardboard and fringed paper.

- Arrange a visit from a local health nurse.

- Keep a record of pupils who lose teeth—including name, date and how and when teeth were lost.

Answers
Teacher check

Curriculum links

Country	Subject	Level	Objectives
England	PSHE	KS 1	• Maintain personal hygiene.
Northern Ireland	PD	KS F	• Recognise and practise basic hygiene skills.
Republic of Ireland	SPHE	Infants	• Recognise and practise basic hygiene skills; e.g. taking proper care of teeth.
Scotland	Health	Level A	• Show an awareness of ways of keeping healthy; e.g. brushing teeth.
Wales	PSE	KS 1	• Know how humans keep healthy.

About your teeth

Children have 20 teeth. You lose teeth and get new ones.

1 How many teeth have you lost? _____

2 Number these teeth from 1 to 20.

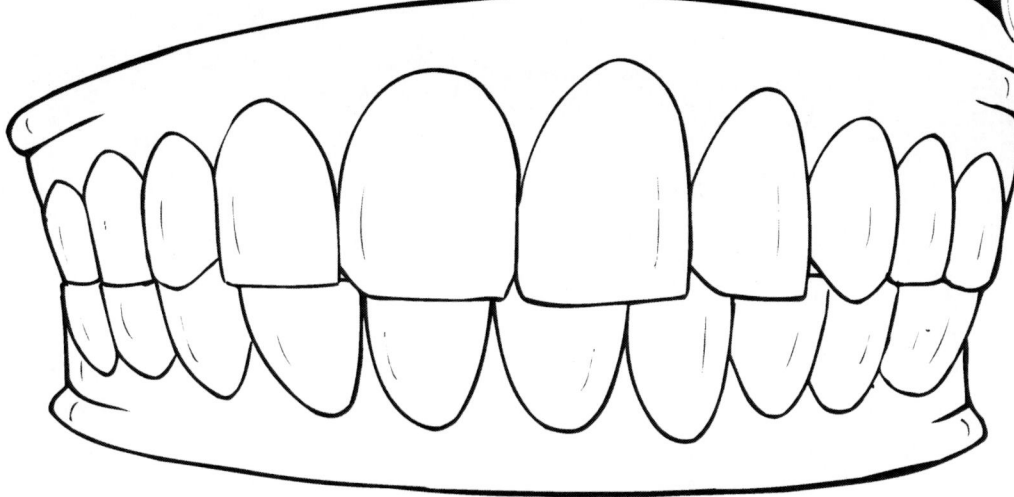

3 Draw two things you do to keep your teeth healthy.

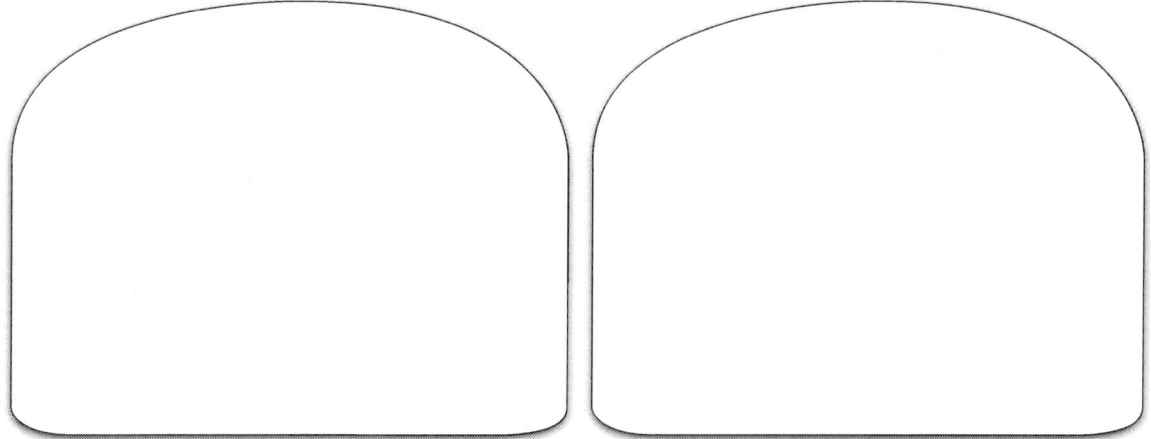

4 Glue pictures of things you use to keep your teeth clean.

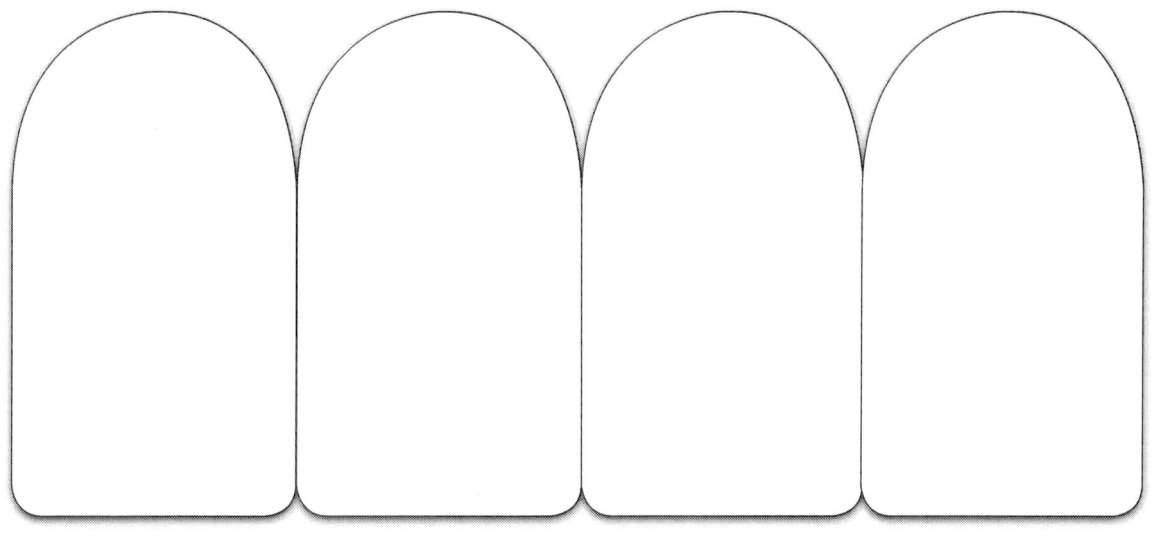

Wintertime

Learning area	Objectives
Geography	• Identifies the winter months. • Recognises seasonal changes.

Resources

• *Winter, spring, summer, fall* a rhyme to the tune of *This old man*:

Winter, spring, summer, fall,
There are seasons, four in all,
With a knick knack ...

Weather changes, sun, rain, snow,
Leaves fall down and flowers grow.
With a knick knack ...

Look outside, you will see,
Just what season it will be.
With a knick knack ...

• a collection of winter clothes, materials and posters showing winter weather

Websites

• Winter craft activities:
http://www.dltk-kids.com/crafts/winter
http://www.kidsdomain.com/craft/_winter.html

Lesson plan and organisation

• Sing the seasons rhyme together. Discuss the four seasons. On the board, write the months.

• Discuss how things change for the winter months: clothes worn, food eaten, social and sporting activities, what things they enjoy or dislike about winter and why.

• Make a list of winter words and phrases.

• Pupils complete the worksheet.

Additional activities

• Pupils write short winter poems.

• Pupils work together to produce a winter scene frieze.

• Pupils compile a list of indoor activities for winter evenings or holidays.

• Pupils create a winter collage using pictures cut from magazines.

Answers

Teacher check

Curriculum links

Country	Subject	Level	Objectives
England	Geography	KS 1	• Observe, record and communicate and use geographical vocabulary.
Northern Ireland	Geography	KS F	• Identify similarities and differences; e.g. weather and understand that some things change over time; e.g. seasons.
Republic of Ireland	Geography	Infants	• Distinguish between summer and winter.
Scotland	Society	Level A	• Describe the main types of weather, including seasonal change.
Wales	Geography	KS 1	• Make observations, record information and use geographical terms.

Wintertime

1 Draw two things you use only in winter.

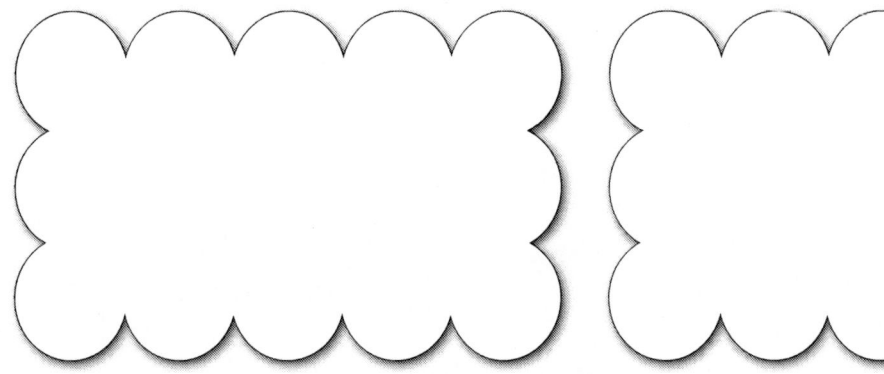

2 Write some winter words.

_____

_____

_____

3 Write the winter months.

_____

_____

_____

4 Draw a picture of things you see only in winter.

5 What do you like about winter?

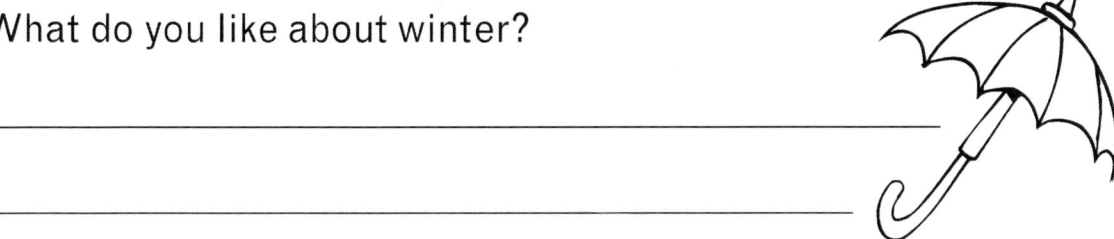

_____

_____

Summertime

Learning area Geography	**Objectives** • Identifies the summer months. • Recognises seasonal changes.

Resources

• *Winter, spring, summer, fall* a rhyme to the tune of *This old man*:

Winter, spring, summer, fall,
There are seasons, four in all,
With a knick knack ...

Weather changes, sun, rain, snow,
Leaves fall down and flowers grow.
With a knick knack ...

Look outside, you will see,
Just what season it will be.
With a knick knack ...

• *Summer* a poem by Mary Ann Hoberman

• a collection of summer clothes, materials and posters showing summer weather

Websites

• summer fun activities:
www.angelfire.com/fl/preschoolfunzone/summerfun.html

www.stormpages.com/cozycottage/summer.html

www.dltk-kids.com/crafts/summer

http://www.kidsdomain.com/craft/_summer.html

Lesson plan and organisation

• Sing the seasons rhyme together. Discuss the four seasons. On the board, write the months.

• Discuss how things change for the summer months: clothes worn, food eaten, social and sporting activities, what things they enjoy or dislike about summer and why.

• Make a list of summer words and phrases.

• Pupils complete the worksheet.

Additional activities

• Pupils write short summer poems.

• Pupils work together to produce a summer scene frieze.

• Pupils compile a list of outdoor activities for summer evenings or holidays.

• Pupils create a summer collage using pictures cut from magazines.

Answers

Teacher check

Curriculum links

Country	Subject	Level	Objectives
England	Geography	KS 1	• Observe, record and communicate and use geographical vocabulary.
Northern Ireland	Geography	KS F	• Identify similarities and differences; e.g. weather and understand that some things change over time; e.g. seasons.
Republic of Ireland	Geography	Infants	• Distinguish between summer and winter.
Scotland	Society	Level A	• Describe the main types of weather, including seasonal change.
Wales	Geography	KS 1	• Make observations, record information and use geographical terms.

The relief teacher toolkit   Prim-Ed Publishing   www.prim-ed.com

Summertime

1 Draw two things you use only in summer.

2 Write some summer words.

_____

_____

_____

3 Write the summer months.

_____

_____

_____

4 Draw a picture of things you see only in summer.

5 What do you like about summer?

_____

_____

The relief teacher toolkit

Then and now

Learning area	
History	

Objectives

- Recognises changes in himself/herself that have occurred over time.
- Appreciates the skills he/she has developed with age and maturity.

Resources

- collection of baby items; e.g. bottle, bib, plastic spoon, dummy, clothes, car seat
- a list of baby games and activities; for example, *Peek-a-boo*

Lesson plan and organisation

- Play some baby games with the pupils. Ask if they still play them now—they may have baby siblings. Make a list on the board of games they used to play as babies but would not play now with their peers.
- Discuss games they play now but would have been unable to play as babies. Make a list of these games. Discuss why they could not have played them as babies.
- Discuss things they used as babies; (for example, dummy, baby bath, rocker, car seat) but do not use now and things they use now they did not use then; (for example, bike, computer, clothing, sports equipment). Consider the reasons why their needs and wants have changed.
- Pupils complete the worksheet.

Additional activities

- Each pupil brings in a photograph of themselves as a baby without letting anyone else see it. Each photograph is given a number. Pupils try to match the photographs with their classmates.
- Make a display of objects used as a baby and used now. On the backing board, pupils write sentences, 'When I was a baby, I used a bath hammock because …'
- Pupils make a personal diary of photographs and milestones in their lives. For this, they will need parental help.

Answers

Teacher check

Curriculum links

Country	Subject	Level	Objectives
England	History	KS 1	• Place events and objects in chronological order and study changes in their own life.
Northern Ireland	History	KS F	• Recognise that people change as they grow and sequence familiar events.
Republic of Ireland	Geography	Infants	• Explore significant personal events; e.g. how I changed as I grew up.
Scotland	Society	Level A	• Demonstrate an awareness of the sequence of events in their own life.
Wales	History	KS 1	• Sequence events and objects and study changes in their own life.

The relief teacher toolkit   Prim-Ed Publishing   www.prim-ed.com

Then and now

1 Draw three things you used only when you were a baby.

2 Draw three things you use now.

3 What can you do?

	I did this when I was a baby.		I do this now.	
	yes	no	yes	no
suck a dummy				
roll over				
make a cake				
ride a bike				
drive a car				
smile				

4 Draw or tell about something special you can do now.

Learning area
Geography

Objectives
• Learns that there is a logic behind spatial planning.
• Learns about the features which occupy a space.

Resources
• big book *Special places at school,* Alphaworld, Gardner Education

Lesson plan and organisation
• Look at the big book and highlight the features of the school layout.

• Take a walk around the school and consider why things are where they are; e.g. bins, paths, toilets.

• Look around the classroom. Make a list of all the permanent furniture. Consider whether it is currently in the best place. Pupils may suggest possible alternatives but must explain the benefits of any changes.

• Study the classroom layout on the worksheet and consider possible places for each item to be added. Explain that the view they see is from above, just as a spider high on the wall might see!

• Pupils draw the items on the plan and answer the questions.

Additional activities
• Pupils draw the current layout of their classroom. Count items.

• Pupils find out from parents and grandparents what furniture they had in their classrooms and how they were laid out. Ask parents and grandparents to draw simple plans. Discuss the differences.

• Each pupil draws a plan of one room in his/her house.

Answers
1. Teacher check
2. 24
3. Teacher check

Curriculum links

Country	Subject	Level	Objectives
England	Geography	KS 1	• Make maps and plans.
Northern Ireland	Geography	KS F	• Use simple maps and drawings.
Republic of Ireland	Geography	Infants	• Use simple drawings of areas; e.g. classroom.
Scotland	Society	Level A	• Develop the mental map of familiar places by identifying main features on a simple map.
Wales	Geography	KS 1	• Make maps and plans.

A classroom

1 Draw these things in the classroom.

1 computer   1 teacher's table   2 cupboards   1 large mat   1 television   2 sport boxes

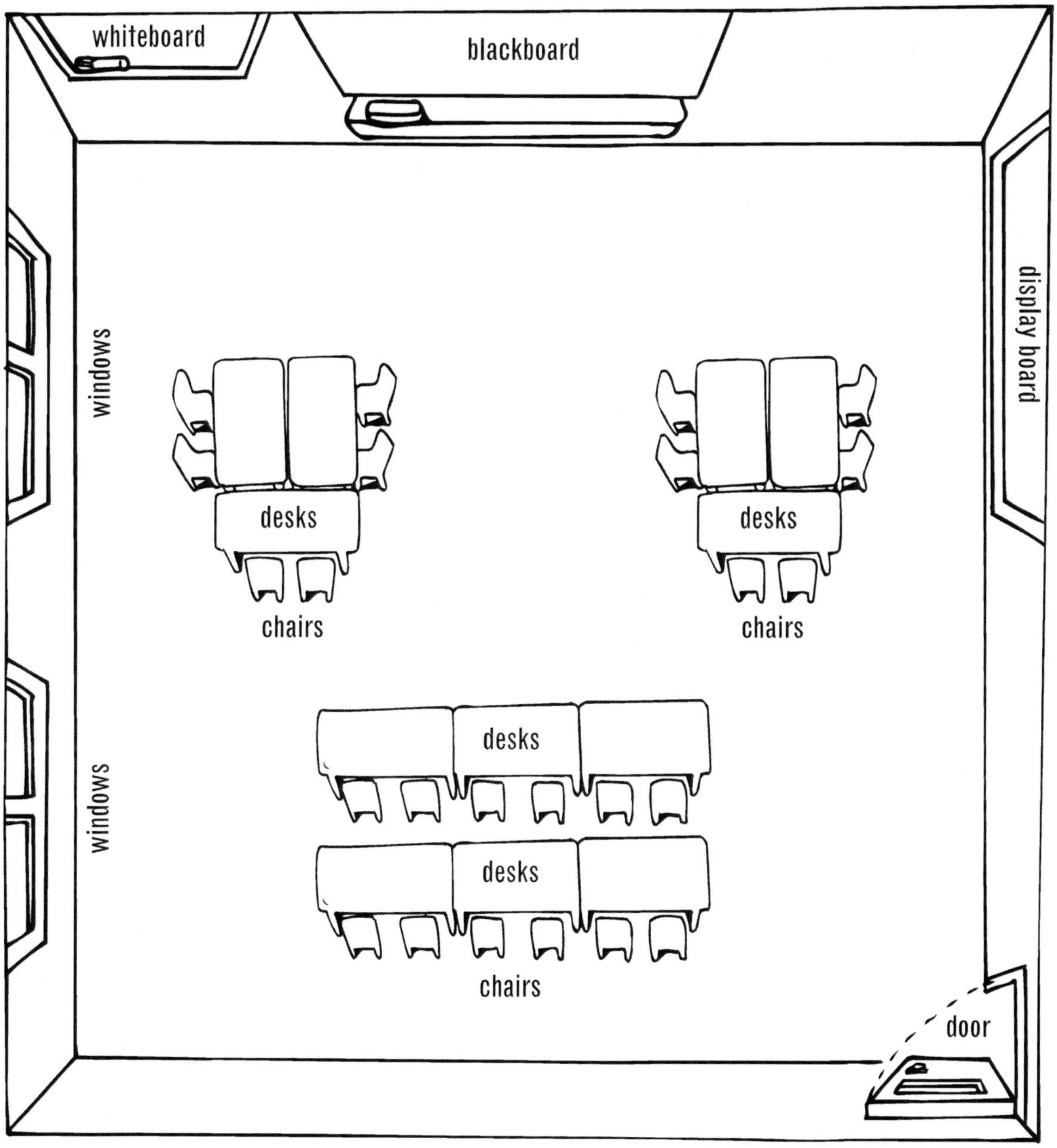

whiteboard   blackboard

windows

display board

desks   desks

chairs   chairs

windows

desks

desks

chairs

door

2 How many children can sit in this room? _____

3 How many children are in your room? _____

Build a pumpkin house

Learning area
Design and technology

Objective
• Develops ideas for designs.

Resources

• *Peter, Peter pumpkin eater*, a traditional rhyme:

Peter, Peter pumpkin eater,
Had a wife but could not keep her.
Put her in a pumpkin shell,
There he kept her very well.

Lesson plan and organisation

• Repeat the rhyme a few times with the pupils.

• Explain that Peter's wife wanted a nice house so he made her one from a pumpkin shell. She was very happy with her new home.

• There are no instructions on the pupil page as they would detract from the finished piece of work.

• Pupils write the name of the rhyme at the top of the page. Discuss the best position for the additions to the house. Pupils place all pictures before gluing them. They colour the picture and draw further additions if they wish.

Additional activities

• Pupils may use the back of the worksheet to draw the inside of the pumpkin house.

• Draw pictures of a house they would like, including garden area.

• Draw a picture of unusual objects as a house; e.g. a boot as in *The old woman who lived in a shoe*. Pupils may draw one from a story or rhyme or make up one of their own.

• Glue the completed pumpkin houses to form a 'street' of pumpkin houses.

Curriculum links

Country	Subject	Level	Objectives
England	DT	KS 1	• Communicate their ideas.
Northern Ireland	Technology	KS F	• Solve a problem.
Republic of Ireland	Science	Infants	• Talk about a plan and communicate it to others.
Scotland	Technology	Level A	• Talk about what might be done to solve a practical problem.
Wales	DT	KS 1	• Make simple decisions and record their ideas.

Build a pumpkin house

Design a building

Learning area
Design and technology

Objectives
• Considers how to build a structure from bricks.
• Describes the structure made.

Resources

• set of large building bricks, enough for 20 for each pupil

• digital camera (optional)

• *Here is a house,* a traditional action rhyme:

Here is a house, built up high,
With two tall chimneys reaching the sky.
Here are the windows. Here is the door.
If we peep inside, we see a mouse on the floor.

• *Here's a house,* another traditional action rhyme:

Here's a house with a floor, with a floor, with a floor.
Here's a house with a wall, with a wall, with a wall.
Here's a house with a roof, with a roof, with a roof.
(Blow the house down.)
There's no house anymore, anymore.
There's no house anymore!

Lesson plan and organisation

• Sing the rhymes and perform the actions. Talk about what is needed when building a house.

• Ask pupils to make a building using the bricks. Allow time to experiment before they choose their final design. Take a photograph of their final structure.

• Pupils complete the worksheet. They only draw one of each type of block used.

• If a digital camera is used, a printed photograph of their building may be glued to the sheet.

• Pupils talk about their structure before attempting to write. Ask questions to help them; e.g. How many layers does it have? How many bricks did you use?

Additional activities

• Pupils count bricks to see who used the most and least bricks.

• In pairs, pupils make up stories about their buildings. What are they? (castles, haunted houses, schools, fire stations ... etc.)

Answers

Teacher check

Curriculum links

Country	Subject	Level	Objectives
England	DT	KS 1	• Communicate their ideas, make models and evaluate their work.
Northern Ireland	Technology	KS F	• Use drawings, models and digital photography to record what they have made.
Republic of Ireland	Science	Infants	• Make simple objects and evaluate and talk about their work.
Scotland	Technology	Level A	• Use given resources to carry out a task and comment on the outcome of their work.
Wales	DT	KS 1	• Design and make products and record their ideas.

The relief teacher toolkit   Prim-Ed Publishing www.prim-ed.com

Design a building

1. Does it stand up well? _____

2. Draw the blocks used.

3. Draw your building.

4. Do you like it? ◯ Yes ◯ No

5. Tell about your building. _____

_____

_____

_____

Wax resist butterflies

Learning area
Art

Objectives
• Experiments with different media.
• Studies patterns in nature.

Resources
• art materials: watercolour paint, large paint brushes, 1 ice-cream container per group, wax crayons, art paper, newspaper, water
• pictures of butterflies
• *The caterpillar,* a poem by Christina Rossetti
• *Fuzzy, wuzzy, creepy crawly,* a poem by Lilian Schulz
• *Crayons,* a poem by Helen H Moore

Websites
• More wax resist ideas: http://www.apfs.org.uk/apfsresources. php?choice=3

Lesson plan and organisation
• Show pupils the pictures of butterflies. Discuss the symmetry of the patterns on the wings. Demonstrate how to draw a large butterfly.
• Pupils design the pattern for their butterfly's wings on the worksheet.

• Pupils use wax crayons to draw the butterfly, with matching patterns on the wings, onto art paper.
• In the ice-cream container, make sufficient watercolour paint for each pupil in the group.
• Using the large paintbrush, demonstrate how the paint is applied, using long strokes across the top of the page to the bottom and leave paintings to dry.
• The worksheet may be stapled to the back of the completed artwork.

Additional activities
• Pupils study the lifecycle of a butterfly.
• Pupils look in detail at the body parts of a butterfly.
• From magazines, pupils cut pictures of butterflies and make a montage.

Answers
Teacher check

Curriculum links

Country	Subject	Level	Objectives
England	Art and design	KS 1	• Record from observation and use a range of materials and processes.
Northern Ireland	Art and design	KS F	• Observe and respond to things they see, talk about colours and patterns and use a range of media and processes.
Republic of Ireland	Visual arts	Infants	• Make drawings based on real experiences and discover colour and pattern in colourful objects.
Scotland	Art and design	Level A	• Draw and paint observed objects.
Wales	Art	KS 1	• Record from observation and make images using a range of materials and processes.

Wax resist butterflies

1 Write a title for your painting.

_____

Draw your butterfly here

2 Name the colours you used. _____

_____

3 Did the butterfly look like one you saw? ◯ Yes ◯ No

4 Tick one box to tell about your butterfly painting.

great   **good**   **ok**   **messy**

Shape collage

Learning area	Objectives
Art	• Practises manipulative skills.
	• Considers what supplementary material is required to complement his/her work.

Resources

- coloured paper for cutting up
- 2-D shapes for tracing around
- magazines with lots of pictures
- card to glue pictures onto
- white paper cut into 1-cm strips

Lesson plan and organisation

- Pupils experiment with making pictures with 2-D shapes. They need to consider the theme of their final piece of work, with the shape picture as the main focus and magazine cuttings as background. At this point, they may think of a title for their work.

- Using the coloured paper, they draw round the shapes and then cut them out. They place and then glue the shapes onto card.

- From the magazines, pupils cut out pictures and scenes to glue onto their work; e.g. if the shape picture is a dog, they may choose a child, grass and trees from a magazine and call their work, 'At the park with Rover'.

- When the picture is complete, pupils write the title of their work on a strip of white paper. This is then glued to the top or bottom of the picture.

- Pictures may be displayed back to back across the room over suspended wire with the worksheet stapled to the back. This activity may be completed in conjunction with pages 38 and 39.

Additional activities

- Pupils make shape puppets, joining each shape to the next with a length of wool.

- Pupils choose one shape and make patterns on paper. Colour in the shapes, with no adjacent shapes having the same colour.

Answers

Teacher check

Curriculum links

Country	Subject	Level	Objectives
England	Art and design	KS 1	• Represent observations and ideas to make images, learn about visual elements; e.g. shape and use variety of materials and processes.
Northern Ireland	Art and design	KS F	• Talk about the shapes of what they are investigating and use a range of materials and processes.
Republic of Ireland	Visual arts	Infants	• Show an awareness of shape.
Scotland	Art and design	Level A	• Explore a range of media and make simple compositions.
Wales	Art	KS 1	• Make images using a range of materials and processes and explore shape.

Shape collage

1 Write a title for your picture.

_____

2 Draw the things you used to make your picture.

3 Draw a sketch of your picture.

4 Tick one box to tell about your picture.

great	**good**	**ok**	**messy**

My home/My toys

Theme	Objectives
Myself	• Describes his/her home and toys accurately.
Learning area	• Considers what makes home/toys special.
English	

Resources

• *The little mouse*, a traditional finger rhyme:

There's such a little, tiny mouse,
(Indicate how small he is.)
Living safely in my house.
(Finger inserted into clenched fist.)
Out at night, he'll softly creep,
(Creep fingers across the floor.)
When everyone is fast asleep.
(Rest head on hands.)
But always in the light of day,
(Use arms to show the sun rising.)
He'll softly, softly creep away.
(Creep fingers back again.)

• *In my toyshop*, a rhyme to the tune of *Here we go round the mulberry bush*:

What have I got in my toyshop today,
Toyshop today, toyshop today?
What have I got in my toyshop today?
You tell me!
(Point to a child who has to mime or describe a toy.)

• Toys from home (optional)

• Photographs of houses (optional)

Lesson plan and organisation

• These activities may be done as two separate lessons, concentrating on one theme at a time.

• Use the rhymes as an introduction to each subject.

• If pupils have brought in photographs of their homes or some of their toys, ask them to talk about them and write any useful words on the board.

• Consider that 'home' is not just about the house but who lives there and the things they do together as a family. Remember also that some toys may have sentimental value. Even when children are too big for them, these toys will always be treasured.

• Give pupils time to discuss, in small groups, what they will write. They write a draft copy and have it checked, before copying it on to the sheet.

Additional activities

• 'My home' sheets may be displayed on a large backing sheet in the shape of a house, with photographs of pupils' houses attached around the edges.

• 'My toys' sheets may be displayed on large backing sheets in the shape of toys; e.g. teddy bear, train, ball.

• Read about homes around the world.

• Allow pupils to explain how some toys work and place them in a 'toy collection' display.

Answers

Teacher check

Curriculum links

Country	Subject	Level	Objectives
England	English	KS 1	• Write in a range of forms.
Northern Ireland	Language and literacy	KS F	• Use a range of writing forms.
Republic of Ireland	English	Infants	• Write about things he/she likes.
Scotland	English	Level A	• Write about personal experience.
Wales	English	KS 1	• Write in a range of forms.

My home

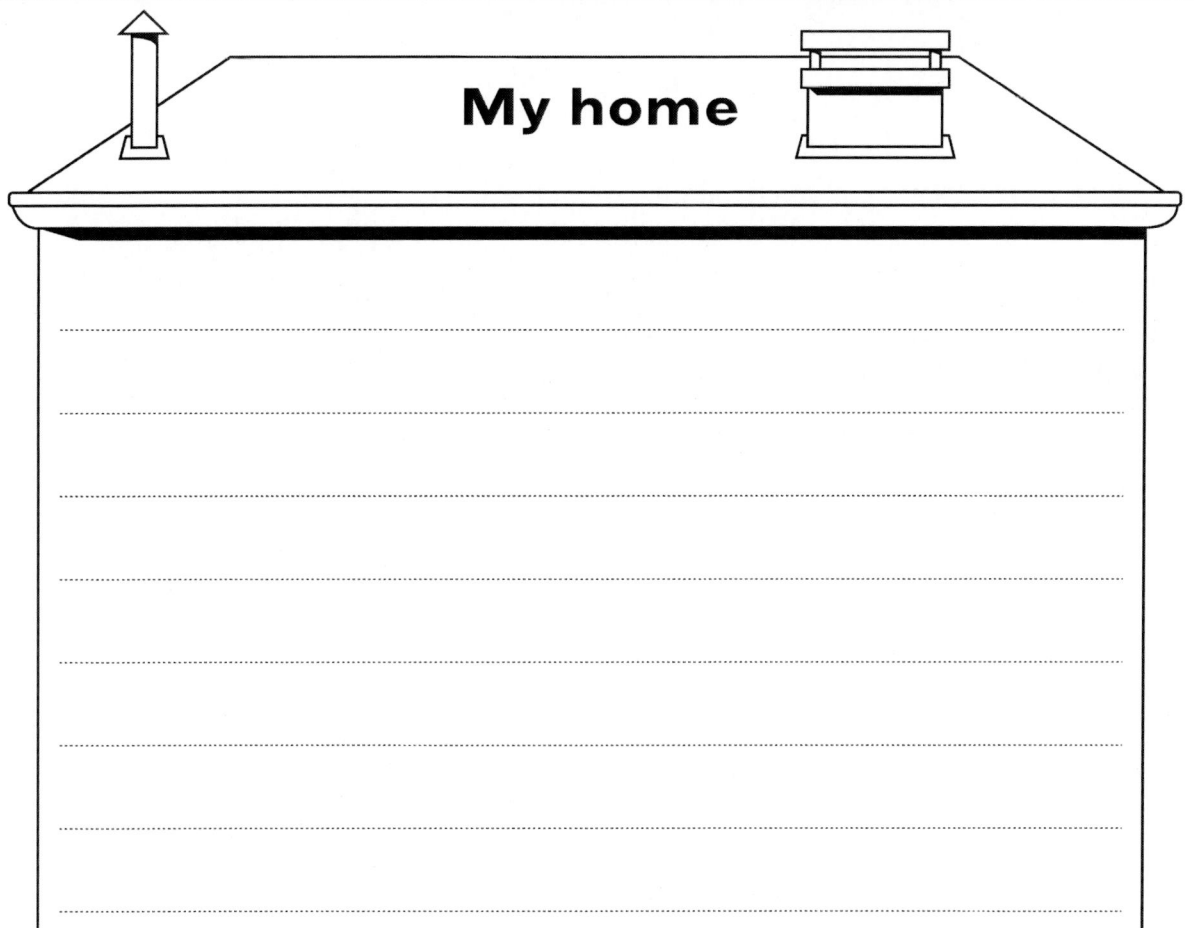

My toys

Body numbers

Theme
Myself

Learning areas
English and mathematics

Objectives
- Knows major body parts.
- Matches picture of body part to written word.

Resources

- large poster of boy and girl with major body parts labelled

- *Head, shoulders, knees and toes*, a traditional rhyme:

  Head, shoulders, knees and toes.
  Knees and toes.
  Head, shoulders, knees and toes,
  Knees and toes.

  And eyes and ears and mouth and nose,
  Head, shoulders, knees and toes,
  Knees and toes.

- *One finger, one thumb, keep moving*, a traditional rhyme:

  One finger, one thumb, keep moving. (x3)
  We'll all be merry and bright.

  One finger, one thumb, one arm, keep moving. (x3)
  We'll all be merry and bright.

  One finger, one thumb, one arm,
  one leg, keep moving. (x3)
  We'll all be merry and bright.

  One finger, one thumb, one arm, one leg,
  one nod of the head, keep moving. (x3)
  We'll all be merry and bright.

  One finger, one thumb, one arm, one leg,
  one nod of the head, stand up, sit down,
  keep moving. (x3)
  We'll all be merry and bright.

Lesson plan and organisation

- Introduce the lesson by performing the rhymes with actions, together.

- Discuss the main role of each body part. Write the names on the board and discuss how many of each we all have. Pupils complete Question 1 on the sheet.

- Pupils carefully trace around one of their hands and complete the rest of the sheet.

Additional activities

- Pupils learn short poems or songs about each body part.

- Measure things around the room using hand spans and footsteps. Discuss why pupils get different answers when measuring the same things. Explain the need for standard measuring units.

- Measure who has the longest arm span, hand span or stride.

Answers

1. 10, 2, 2, 2, 2, 4, 20

2. Teacher check

Curriculum links

Country	Subject	Level	Objectives
England	Maths	KS 1	• Count objects reliably.
Northern Ireland	Maths and numeracy	KS F	• Count objects.
Republic of Ireland	Maths	Infants	• Count objects in a set.
Scotland	Maths	Level A	• Count.
Wales	Maths	KS 1	• Count objects reliably.

Body numbers

1 Write the number or number words.

👉 I have _____ fingers.

👁 I have _____ eyes.

I have _____ legs.

✋ I have _____ feet.

👂 I have _____ ears.

I have _____ hands and feet.

I have _____ fingers and toes.

2 (a) Trace around your hand.

(b) Draw your fingernails.

(c) Write your name on the hand.

(d) How many letters does your name have?

_____

The relief teacher toolkit

All about me

Theme	
Myself	**Objectives**
Learning areas	• Describes personal things about self and family.
English/Health/ Values	• Acknowledges positive attributes about self.

Resources

• tape measure

• prepare an 'All about me' of a real or imaginary child, the same age as the pupils (optional)

Lesson plan and organisation

• Sit in a circle with the pupils. Each person takes a turn to say one thing about himself/ herself. Choose the topic for each round, using the worksheet as a guide. Write helpful words and phrases on the board.

• Read the 'All about me' you have prepared.

• Pupils complete the worksheet. Pupils may answer 'zero' for the pets, brothers and sisters. Pupils will need help to measure their heights.

• Individual pupils read out their last two sentences to the whole group/class.

Additional activities

• Teacher reads out specific pupil information (without name) and the class tries to guess who it is.

• Pupils read their information to the class as an oral report.

• Complete surveys of favourite foods and TV programmes from the sheets. Display results in different graphical forms.

• Make a whole-class chart of favourite things to do.

Answers

Teacher check

Curriculum links

Country	Subject	Level	Objectives
England	PSHE	KS 1	• To think about themselves and feel positive.
Northern Ireland	PD	KS F	• Explore who they are and their favourite things.
Republic of Ireland	SPHE	Infants	• Appreciate all the features that make a person special and unique and recognise personal preferences.
Scotland	PSD		• Know themselves as unique individuals and express positive thoughts about themselves.
Wales	PSE	KS 1	• Feel positive about themselves.

All about me

❖ My name is _____

_____.

❖ I am _____ years old.

❖ My birthday is on _____

_____.

❖ I have _____ pets at home.

❖ I have _____ brothers and _____ sisters.

❖ I am _____ cm tall.

Glue your picture here

❖ My favourite food is _____.

❖ My favourite TV shows are _____

_____.

❖ My teacher's name is _____.

❖ The best thing about me is _____

_____

_____

_____

_____.

❖ My favourite things to do are _____

_____.

My body

Theme	Objectives

Theme
Myself

Learning areas
Science/Health

Objectives
- Knows the major body parts.
- Matches picture of body part to written word.
- Understands the value of healthcare.

Resources

- collection of products used to care for our bodies; e.g. toothpaste, soap, sunscreen
- large poster of boy and girl with major body parts labelled (optional)
- *Head, shoulders, knees and toes*, a traditional rhyme:

  Head, shoulders, knees and toes.
  Knees and toes.
  Head, shoulders, knees and toes,
  Knees and toes.

  And eyes and ears and mouth and nose,
  Head, shoulders, knees and toes,
  Knees and toes.

- big book about the human body

Lesson plan and organisation

- Introduce the lesson by performing the rhyme with actions.
- Use the big book or poster showing the body parts and words for pupils to recognise. Say a body part and ask a pupil to point to the word in the book. Repeat until all parts have been mentioned.
- Pupils can copy, write or cut out and glue the names of the body parts in the correct boxes.

- Talk about ways in which we look after our bodies, from personal hygiene to protection from the sun and other elements. Make lists of the things we need to do to look after our hair, teeth, skin, nails. How do we use these things? Discuss why we need to look after our personal hygiene. What happens if we do not? This area requires a sensitive approach.
- Pupils complete Question 2.

Additional activities

- Pupils perform mimes of a healthcare activity; e.g. brushing their teeth, washing their hair. Encourage them to include each step; e.g. picking up the toothpaste, removing the cap, picking up the brush.
- Pupils choose one part of the body and design a poster about how to look after it.
- Using pictures from magazines, pupils produce a montage of healthcare products.
- Pupils draw round the outline of one pupil. Make labels on the computer with arrows to match to the outline.

Answers

Teacher check

Curriculum links

Country	Subject	Level	Objectives
England	PSHE	KS 1	• Know the names of the main parts of the body and how to improve their health and well-being.
Northern Ireland	PD	KS F	• Be aware of how to care for his/her own body in order to keep it healthy and well.
Republic of Ireland	SPHE	Infants	• Name parts of the human body and understand how to care for his/her own body in order to keep it healthy and well.
Scotland	Science/ Health	Level A	• Name the main external parts of the human body and show an awareness of how to keep healthy.
Wales	PSE	KS 1	• Name the main parts of the human body and know how to keep the body healthy.

My body

1 Copy the labels into the correct boxes.

hand	toe	arm	finger
knee	neck	leg	face

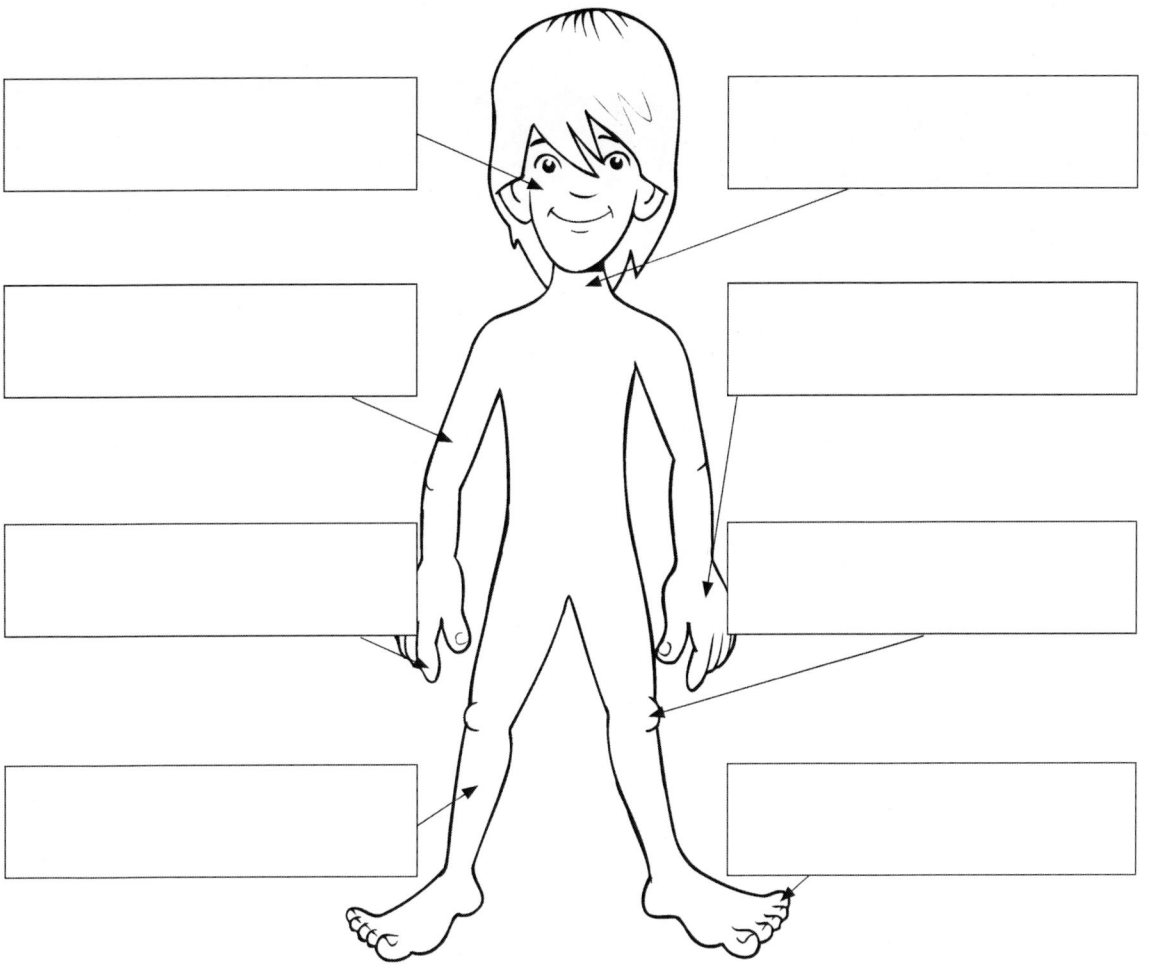

2 Draw pictures to show things we use to care for ...

(a) our teeth.   (b) our body in the sun.

Things I like

Theme	Objectives
Myself	• Recognises the differences that exist between individuals.
Learning area	• Expresses personal preferences.
Values	

Resources

- magazines and store catalogues

Lesson plan and organisation

- Worksheet should be enlarged to A3 size to allow room for pictures.

- Discuss favourite things with the class. Divide the board into four sections and write headings from the sheet. Write words and phrases appropriate to each as directed by the pupils. Simple pictures may be drawn as well as the words for those pupils less able to read.

- In groups, pupils look through magazines and choose pictures to cut out and glue onto their sheets. Three items on each section would be sufficient. If they cannot find a picture to represent a favourite item, they can draw it themselves.

- Pupils discuss the content of their sheets.

Additional activities

- Pupils choose one item from their sheet and present a mini-topic, describing the item in more detail; e.g. 'My favourite food is pizza'. Describe the process of making a pizza, preparing and layering the toppings on the base, how long it takes to cooks, how to cut it.

- Categorise the items in each section; e.g. favourite toys: by material, size, powered/unpowered.

- Discuss a healthy lifestyle in terms of favourite food and games.

- Make a 'Things I like' chart by cutting the sheets into the four sections and putting all the 'toys', 'food', 'animals' and 'games' together. Remind pupils to write their names on each section.

Answers

Teacher check

Curriculum links

Country	Subject	Level	Objectives
England	PSHE	KS 1	• To think about themselves and recognise what they like.
Northern Ireland	PD	KS F	• Explore who they are and their favourite things.
Republic of Ireland	SPHE	Infants	• Recognise and record personal preferences.
Scotland	PSD		• Know themselves as unique individuals.
Wales	PSE	KS 1	• Feel positive about themselves and express their own ideas.

Things I like

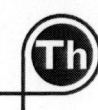

Cut and paste or draw.

My favourite toys	My favourite food
My favourite animals	**My favourite games**